D1522015

THE RETRIEVER GAME

THE
RETRIEVER
GAME

Boyd Gibbons

STACKPOLE
BOOKS

Copyright © 1992 by Boyd Gibbons

Published by
STACKPOLE BOOKS
Cameron and Kelker Streets
P.O. Box 1831
Harrisburg, PA 17105

Printed in the United States of America

First Edition

10 9 8 7 6 5 4 3 2 1

Cover painting by Thomas Quinn of FC – AFC Suncrest Tasmanian, owned by M.J. Mowinckle .

Library of Congress Cataloging-in-Publication Data

Gibbons, Boyd
      The retriever game / Boyd Gibbons
          p.   cm.
      ISBN 0-8117-1192-7
      1. Retrievers.   2. Retrievers—Training.   3. Field trials.
      I. Title.
      SF429.R4G53   1992
      636.7'52—dc20   92-8521
                                                                CIP

To John Rosenberg

$\mathcal{W}$ELL BEFORE dawn on a mid-November morning in 1988, an unusual caravan of customized pickup trucks began arriving at the Stardust ranch in southern Oklahoma. They had pulled out of a parking lot at a shopping mall in Duncan, moved slowly down the main drag of town past the contemporary middens of the plains—Ronnie's Auto Parts, Daylight Donuts, Taco Tico—and out into cattle country. Interspersed among the trucks were vans, station wagons, and a few elephantine RVs, but the pickups predominated, their beds boxed professionally in aluminum and stainless steel. At that dark hour they appeared to be nothing more than campers, but they were dog trucks. On straw and cedar shavings inside these mobile kennels were a half dozen Golden Retrievers, possibly a Chesapeake on vacation, and in greatest number Labradors, the prevailing dogs of retriever field trials. They had come to compete for six days in the most demanding trial of working retrievers: the National Championship Stake.

Pitching over the rolling terrain, the first headlights reached the perimeter of the gallery—a blue nylon rope run through the coiled ends of reinforcing rods driven into the ground. Beyond this remuda somewhere in the dark, there was some shouting and playing of flashlights as the officials searched for the line, the fixed spot from which the handlers would send their dogs.

In the middle of the motorcade was a cocoa brown, three-quarter ton Sierra Classic driven by John J. Sweezey of Chestertown, Maryland, a man who is not inclined to run with the pack. Jay Sweezey's GMC was pulling a low breadbox trailer—a fourteen-hole Scott box, fifteen thousand dollars delivered—its shiny sides patterned with small louvered doors. The kennel interiors behind the doors were stainless steel, because urine and saliva corrode aluminum, and Sweezey doesn't care to see his black Labs dulled gray with aluminum oxide. The kennels were insulated and snug, with fans drawing air to the dogs through the louvers, which blocked their view. At field trials, competing retrievers are not permitted to watch the tests before coming to the line. Among the fourteen expectant Labs that Sweezey was hauling, two had qualified for this National. Long before the convoy formed he had aired them all in the city park.

Sweezey swung wide of the assembled vehicles and parked away from the crowd. He propped up doors on either side of the trailer exposing the breezeways, two large openings that helped give more air to his dogs. Jay Sweezey is a big, powerful man heralded by a trombone voice. At sixty-four, he still has hair as brown as his truck. He is outdoors nearly all year, his eyes in a perpetual squint. His broad shoulders and iron arms seem to tilt him forward as he walks, suggesting someone who could clear out bars.

Sweezey's dogs were compliantly silent. Barking dogs are at the head of a long list of aggravations for which his patience is decisively short. Retrievers that bark or whine while on line at a field trial are penalized, and if they persist, they are eliminated.

I once shared a motel room with Sweezey at the Swampdog trial near Dillsburg, Pennsylvania, when a stock car race had jammed every motel and he offered me a spare bed. The field trial headquarters was at another motel. Jay Sweezey is a sociable man, but he prefers not to overnight where the other trialers collect. "There's always some jackass with a single dog. He's got an entire parking lot to air him, and so he lets that sonofabitch piss on my tires. My dogs go nuts."

Sweezey had parked his rig as close as possible to the room. That night a couple of the Labs in his trailer decided to commune openly with Dillsburg.

"I don't put up with that crap," Sweezey said, rising from his bed. He threw open the door and bellowed, "QUIET!" The barking immediately stopped, as, I expect, did all conversation within a mile of greater Dillsburg. Sweezey stood barefoot in his white boxer shorts, filling the open doorway and throwing a shadow of alien proportions across the macadam. Among the gear in his trailer was an electric cattle prod. It was not difficult to imagine two thoroughly intimidated Labradors trying to squint through the louvers at this imposing, backlit figure and hoping for all their lives that there would be no forward movement. Sweezey shut the door and fell asleep on his back.

Jay Sweezey is a professional retriever trainer and handler, polishing and running his clients' dogs at field trials. He has been "playing with dogs" since 1948. Early in his career he left Great South Bay of Long Island for the Eastern Shore of the Chesapeake Bay, where for a number of years he ran pheasant shoots and trained retrievers for a former commodore of the New York Yacht Club. Since then he has worked dogs for various people of circumstance, including Forrest Mars (candy), Mrs. Albert Loening (aircraft), Rosamond Chubb (insurance), and currently Bill and Ginny Atterbury, who divide their time between Sun Valley, Idaho, and Palm City, Florida.

Sweezey is a pro, as they say, of the old school, with a fondness for appropriate clothes: Stafford's plantation-cotton pants and pull-on Russell boots. Although not wealthy himself, he regrets that old money no longer influences the manners at field trials and that tweed and flannel (and a good deal more) have disappeared from trials with the decline of Abercrombie & Fitch and the ascendancy of denim.

"You go to a trial today," Sweezey says, "and it looks like a plumbers' convention. In the old days everyone wore ties."

Sweezey was in his sage green ensemble of matching cotton trousers and cap. The L. L. Bean cap was unadorned, except that on the crown just over the bill he had sewn a small bow of yellow grosgrain ribbon. The bows are something of a Sweezey trademark. Each day of the National he would appear in a different combination: a yellow bow on a green cap, a bright green bow on tan, brown on tan, white on blue, blue on white. On the following Saturday, in slanting rain, he would change caps three times. I did not, however, see him wear the blue cap distributed by the National Retriever Club, which featured the seal of Oklahoma (a Comanche shield, peace pipe, and sprig of laurel) surrounded by white letters announcing "National Retriever Championship Duncan, OK, 1988." He does not abide being someone else's billboard.

"I always have different caps—I like hats—but I hate those damned caps with things written all over them. It's so ostentatious. You see guys with their kennel names on the sides of their trucks. I have only my initials on the doors."

The initials were half an inch high above a small painting of a woodcock. Sweezey carries his ties for evening parties in a zippered cloth case. His sportcoats are often tailored English wools, his travel bags from Gokey of St. Paul—leather and green canvas, soft from years and miles of travel. A small, oblong brass plate is riveted to the bags. "J. J. Sweezey, Chestertown, MD."

Sweezey reached into the cab behind the seat for his white jacket. Under hunting conditions, a retriever is usually working close enough to the gun to pick up hand signals directing him to a fallen bird he didn't see. But the competition at field trials has led to retrieves a quarter mile away and even farther. When sent over such distances on a "blind" retrieve (one with a bird that the dog isn't allowed to see planted), a dog running off course and whistled to a stop must be able to pick out his handler for directions from among the crowd and confusion of vehicles. A white coat stands out. Even the guns wear white so that the dogs can orient the "marks" (the birds they are allowed to see). Sweezey's coat is an extra large, from Lucky Dog, a functional dinner jacket without lapels. The original patch pockets were too small, so he ripped them off and shipped the coat to Thomasville, Georgia, with instructions for Stafford's to sew on something big and durable enough to hold his leather leads, his chain collars, his stuff. The replacement pockets were ocher canvas—capacious marsupia.

"You know where I got this idea? Captain Kangaroo. He always had those big coat pockets."

There have been ten generations of Sweezeys on Long Island. His grandfather, who sailed Great South Bay, introduced Jay's father to the traditions of duck shooting—canvasbacks, redheads, scaup. Sweezey's father, a conductor for the Long Island Railroad who on occasion during Prohibition was known to turn out a passable corn whiskey, had a consummate knack for building duck boats and for constructing decoys of icebox cork. He used clothespins for the bills.

"By bicycle we lived only ten minutes from the ducking marsh," Sweezey said. "Times were tough, and shells were hard to get. A duck was like a roast turkey. It was meat hunting, over bait. We were dropping a half ton of corn out there every week. We'd let the ducks swim into the rig and sluice six or seven on the water. Sport hunting came later. My dad had Chesapeakes, and in those days when you'd shoot a duck, your dog would get it and drop it on the shore. That was considered pretty good retrieving.

"When this trial game started, you were looking for a dog you could shoot over."

Sweezey slipped a white bib with the black numerals 56 over his head. He got out a big water dish for his dogs and filled it from the trailer spigot. He had some time before his first retriever would be called to the line.

Some weeks before the National, Sweezey had finished the season's eastern trials and headed west. He had run the Bluegrass in Lexington, stopped in Memphis to ship a dog back to its owner in Boston, and rolled on to his son Kent's kennels north of Dallas to train for this culminating event that had brought so many retrievers to Duncan. Sweezey had been running retrievers in field trials longer than anyone on the circuit. He had competed in more than two dozen Nationals, a bridesmaid finalist more times than he cared to remember. The trophy had always eluded him.

In the brains of dogs there resides an irresistible urge to chase down prey. Terriers prefer mice and rats, greyhounds course after rabbits, and a cat seems to raise the level of adrenaline in them all. This has not been lost on generations of hunters, who have channeled that instinct in the sporting breeds—the retrievers, pointers, setters, and spaniels—into the pursuit of gamebirds for the table.

As dogs are the elaborate extensions of their owners' egos, it was only a matter of time until a group of Englishmen decided in 1865 to see who had the best hunting dog by testing them in competition in the field.

About that time in Tennessee a man by the name of P. H. Bryson, who had been shot up in the Civil War and sent home to become a statistic, received some encouraging advice from his physician: Buy yourself a shotgun and a bird dog and go hunting. In the South a bird dog meant one of the pointing breeds—wide-ranging pointers and setters—which, until the Lab got its substantial toehold on this continent in the 1930s, were the popular American hunting dogs. Bryson bought a setter and went after quail. In 1874, his body intact and his enthusiasm for hunting dogs still rising, he organized near Memphis the first field trial in the United States, restricted, understandably enough, to setters and pointers. Retriever competitions did not begin in the United States for more than another half century. (The American Kennel Club also licenses field trials for beagles, basset hounds, dachshunds, and spaniels.)

Of the eighty-two National and National Amateur Retriever Championships held since 1941 and 1957 (the latter limited to amateur handlers, the National open to both pros and amateurs), all but five have been won by Labrador Retrievers. Golden Retrievers have won only one National Amateur and four Nationals. No Chesapeake Bay Retriever has won either.

Why this is so is a subject that divides breeders and trainers as much as it does the dogs. Some say that the sensitive Golden is too much of a lover, the Chessie too independent. There is general agreement that the superior dogs of all three breeds are easy to train but that the breeding pools of both Chessies and Goldens are small compared to the sea of competitive Labs. Few Chessies show up at retriever field trials; some Goldens will be in the running; but the reigning dog is the one with the brown eyes and slick black (or yellow) coat: the versatile, driving Labrador Retriever.

Hamilton Rowan, a springer spaniel man who was for many years the director of field trials for the American Kennel Club, believes that the Labrador has dominated retriever trials because it can endure the punishment of the training. "A Golden can't take that kind of training, nor a Chessie. You keep firing electricity into a Chessie and he's going to come back and take your hand off. It isn't that the Lab is a better dog—he just has a different temperament and can take it. Of course, a Lab person would hang you from a tree if you said that to him."

Rex Carr, who has probably trained more National and National Amateur retriever champions than anyone, is prepared to get out the rope. "The principal difference between retriever breeds is not as Hamilton Rowan expressed it. Labradors haven't dominated field trials because they can take the punishment of training—it's because of their retrieving instinct and desire."

Torch Flinn of Greenwich, Connecticut, has been breeding and trialing Goldens for forty-five years. "I think Goldens are easier to train than Labs, but good Goldens are rarer than good Labs. Goldens have been poorly bred for so long. What they have is eye appeal, that soft look. They're so popular, and so many people breed for money, that the breeders are afraid to lose the looks. In field trials, marking is of paramount importance. You can teach dogs to handle, but you can't teach them to mark birds. They have to have it in their genes. Good marking is not common in Goldens. Most of them are looking around and want to be patted."

Jackie Mertens, whose Top Brass Cotton was the only Golden to have won the National Amateur, was frustrated. If her next litter of Goldens didn't turn out— she had been raising and training Goldens for twenty-five years—she would consider going to Labs. "There aren't more Goldens in field trials because they can't hold a candle to the Labs. You can get a good Lab with almost every puppy you buy. The Lab has a more stable personality. The Goldens are more aggressive toward other dogs—they want to chew them up. The Goldens' inability to take correction gets in the way of their thought processes and makes them very difficult to train. When you start putting pressure on them, their minds get so frazzled that the burning desire to retrieve just isn't there. Some of them are so worried before you send them, so upset sitting on line, they can't get that picture and look out. Chesapeakes? They make the Goldens look good."

This would bring Dyane Baldwin out of her chair. She is a Chessie woman, and Chessie people stick with their dogs. Chesapeake Bay Retrievers were the market hunter's duck dogs—independent, inclement brown dogs that lived under the porch. "In the early duck dogs," she said, "you were looking not for speed but for endurance. The dog was expected to work more on his own, to think through his retrieving situations, go for the cripples first, use his nose. If you want a dog to compete in licensed field trials, you need speed and a dog that will put up with that electronic collar program. The tests in field trials run contrary to the Chessie's independent nature. The Chessie is always thinking for himself rather than your way. They don't fit into the program of the professional trainer who has fifteen, twenty dogs to train and doesn't have the time to give that Chessie the extra attention. The Lab doesn't fight your will as much."

Although early retriever history is considerably murky, the Lab, the Chessie, and possibly the Goldens as well are thought to have had roots in Newfoundland from the dogs used for centuries by Devon fishermen off St. John's. The St. John's dogs rode out in the dories. When cod flopped loose off the hooks, the dogs would jump over the side. The first retrievers retrieved fish.

From the early nineteenth century the Labrador's breeding (and later the Golden's) was managed by the British aristocracy, who had the time, money, and influence to develop a superior retriever. Labs were first bred in England by the second earl of Malmesbury and in Scotland by the fifth duke of Buccleuch. Goldens made their first appearance in a litter when, in 1868, Sir Dudley Marjoribanks, first lord Tweedmouth, purchased in Brighton a "sport"—the yellow progeny of flat-coat and curly-coat retrievers—and bred it to a Tweed Water Spaniel.

By the turn of the twentieth century, the Labrador Retriever had become the preferred dog at shoots in England and Scotland. Today when retrievers go to trial across the kale and beet fields of England, it is no surprise that the Labs of Sandringham House have a place at the line. The kennels at Sandringham House are the kennels of the Queen of England.

An attraction for things British led Americans of influence who had hunted over Labs on driven grouse shoots in Scotland to bring these dogs back with them to their Long Island estates. They brought, as well, Scottish gamekeepers to raise ducks and pheasants for the shoots and to train and handle the dogs. In 1913, W. Averell Harriman hired Tom Briggs for *Arden*. Dave Elliot trained for Jay Carlisle at *Wingan*, Douglas Marshall for the Marshall Fields' kennels at *Caumsett*, Colin MacFarlane for Robert Goulet.

In 1931, as president of the Labrador Retriever Club, Audrey Fields helped organize the first retriever field trial in the United States. It was held at the Goulets' *Glenmere Court*, Chester, New York: eight thousand acres of marsh and field and pen-raised pheasants. Licensed by the AKC, the event was run in the manner of the early English trials, with an advancing line of beaters, three guns with attendants, and two handlers with their dogs at heel. Boys in the ditches threw live pheasants into flight. Guns came to shoulders. The judge directed which dog would make the retrieve. The trial took place on December 21, not because it was on the eve of winter but because it fell on a Monday. There was a strong interest among the sponsors not to attract common spectators to the gallery. The trainers did not eat at the big table, the immovable line between them and their employers dividing class as much as it did function.

The early years of retriever field trials were Long Island social events draped with Loden and tweed from the trunk shows and needle of Maurie Meyers of Philadelphia and Shep Miller of Southampton. There were boots by Gokey, by Russell, high-laced English boots. Burberry bi-swing shooting coats with bellows pockets. Barbour rain gear of Egyptian long-staple cotton that had been boiled in vats of oil and wax. There were wool knickers, gabardine jodhpurs, English cavalry twill and whipcord trousers faced in calfskin, Viyella shirts, silk English ascots, and slouch hats and snap brims so loaded down with trial and club pins it's a wonder the felt didn't collapse.

The competition was loose. Handlers threw stones into the water to show the dogs the duck. A two-stone retrieve beat a three-stone retrieve. As so few dogs were competing, the trial had an intermission for a leisurely lunch. The National Champion was simply the retriever who had accumulated the most points that year at field trials, of which there were few—five in 1935, ten in 1937, twenty in 1940. The idea of a conclusive annual trial to determine the top retriever did not bear fruit until 1941, when the National Retriever Field Trial Club was formed to run the National Championship Stake. Only fifteen retrievers ran in the first National at Penniman's Point, Quogue, Long Island. The trial was over in three days, concluding on the Sunday that Pearl Harbor came under attack.

By the 1988 National in Oklahoma, the field trial game had progressed some distance beyond one-stone retrieves. So many retrievers were competing—eighty-five in all—that the contest ran from before dawn to dusk, Monday through Saturday, opening in Indian summer and finishing in a winter storm. More than time and distance separated this National from the social strata of prewar Long Island. Out on range land unburdened by italics, the handlers wore riveted jeans, the core of a small, insular society of tenaciously competitive trialers and their muscular, athletic dogs.

Some days in advance of the National, the three judges—Dennis Bath, Tony Snow, and Clint Joyner, expenses paid but volunteers all—had hovered in a helicopter over the ranches to be used for the National, making a reconnaissance they considerably expanded on the ground as they set up the tests that the dogs would run. Following them out there was the entire retinue of other volunteers: marshals, traffic and grounds crews, gun teams, bird stewards and throwers with their crates of ring-necked pheasants and mallard ducks. The birds were domestically raised—for restaurants, shooting preserves, and retriever trials. In the crates the pheasants wore blinders, for like chickens they are cannibalistic when confined. When their moment of flight arrived, the blinders would come off.

The judges assessed the Stardust ranch—rolling fields of big bluestem over ragweed, "old field," and buffalo grass. Old field grass grows where not much else will. Oklahomans also refer to it as needle grass; the spears stick in your socks. Quail are inclined toward the ragweed, and they can have it. The bluestem was maroon. Here and there groves of scrub and red oak still hung to their caramel leaves.

For the first test, the judges selected a deeply eroded meadow, placing the line up on the rim. Viewed from this terrace, the test appeared to my untrained eye as deceptively uncomplicated. A little roll to the land maybe, some brush and high weeds—a piece of cake, I thought, for these dogs.

Snow walked down into the wash to see what the dogs would encounter. Although he is the size one might associate with an offensive lineman for the Washington Redskins, he soon disappeared from sight. Eventually he reappeared, considerably smaller, climbed the far hill, and looked back. When he returned, he was breathing hard.

"You know what I think?" he said to Bath. "This is tougher than shit. There's a lot of stuff for them to get lost in. When a dog gets in those low places, he is really going to have trouble."

This place would do fine. It had ample obstacles, and the judges, mindful of the rule books in their pockets, would add enough of their own.

This is the philosophy of the American Kennel Club on retriever field trials:

> The purpose of a Non-Slip Retriever trial is to determine the relative merits of Retrievers in the field. Retriever field trials should, therefore, simulate as nearly as possible the conditions met in an ordinary day's shoot. . . . The function of a Non-Slip Retriever is to seek and retrieve "fallen" game when ordered to do so. He should sit quietly on line or in the blind, walk at heel, or assume any station designated by his handler until sent to retrieve. When ordered, a dog should retrieve quickly and briskly without unduly disturbing too much ground

and should deliver tenderly to hand. He should then await further orders. Accurate marking is of primary importance. A dog which marks the fall of a bird, uses the wind, follows a strong cripple, and will take direction from his handler is of great value.

The AKC rules and advisory committee standing recommendations go on for eighty pages, listing dozens of serious, moderate, and minor faults. A dog that breaks from the line before being sent is out of the trial. He can creep a little (minor fault). He is in trouble if he is reluctant to "enter rough cover, water, ice, or mud" that is "unpleasant going."

On the whole, the judges want to see how well a retriever marks a fall (a visible bird he must retrieve without assistance) and handles to a blind (a hidden bird to which he is directed, or "cast," over great distances by the handler's whistle and arm signals). They assess the dog's adaption to training—steadiness on the line, control, responsiveness to direction from the handler, delivery of the bird—and his natural abilities of memory, intelligence, attention, nose, courage, perseverance, and style.

I asked Snow what he looked for in style.

"Animation, to a certain degree quickness," he said. "But it's mainly a matter of *heart*. These old dogs can't run as fast as the young ones, but if their tails are up and they're happy, they're showing you a lot of heart."

The National is an elimination contest of ten tests, half on land and half in water, a mixture of marks and blinds. A handler who blows his whistle and waves his arms while his dog is working on a mark soon handles himself right out of the National.

These were all seasoned judges, but Dennis Bath, having judged as many trials as the other two combined, was inclined toward command. He does not shrink from confrontations. Twenty-five years ago on the night before his first field trial, Bath's dogs got to barking outside the motel. The next day some guy with circles under his eyes confronted him.

"Were those your goddamned dogs last night?"

"Yeah, and what of it?"

That day Bath went to the line with his dog and discovered that this guy was a judge.

Now setting up the National, Bath was concerned about obstacles beneath his feet: the line was cratered with armadillo holes. "Orlie, could we get someone to fill those up? Someone's going to break a leg up here." Orlie Boehler, the chief marshal, a lawyer from Duncan, did not look entirely comfortable with the pressures of this trial. The grounds crew got out their shovels.

Bath cupped his hands and shouted across the gullies, "All right, guns up!"

The two gun teams—three men each, a thrower and two men cradling shotguns—stood up from their lawn chairs. The judges had decided that the first two tests, a land series, would be a double mark followed by a single blind. The first mark would come from a team standing two hundred yards away, slightly to the left in high grass and brush on a ridge above two stock ponds fringed with willows. The thrower would toss a dead hen pheasant underhand in a long arc to the right as the two men with shotguns beside him fired blank "poppers" in the air: one shot before the throw to get the dog's attention, the other fired at the apogee of bogus flight.

The second team—the "flier" mark—stood lower down the hillside one hundred and twenty yards straight away. Beside them were plastic crates full of clucking pheasants. The thrower here would pitch a live pheasant into the air. The two guns would allow the flier a certain distance of uninterrupted flight, then shoot simultaneously and bring it down. The bird's end would be quick and sure, as the guns, who have shot together for years at these trials, are more than reliable wing shots.

The "blind" bird was planted three hundred yards up the hill to the right.

Bath yelled to the gun team on the left. "Let's see the popper bird!" The thrower threw it underhand into a high arc. Bath squatted at retriever height. A dead tree would obscure the dogs' line of sight to the bird.

"Orlie, could we get someone with a chain saw over there?"

The grounds crew addressed the tree and yanked the cord. It wouldn't start. There was some commotion around the pickup trucks. Another chain saw, nothing. Third chain saw, zilch. Orlie was working himself into a litigious mood. The fourth chain saw started with a snarl. The tree came down.

The second gun team shot some flier pheasants. Bath cupped his hands to his mouth. "That second bird fell just where we want it!" Radio communication established for the throwers and gun teams the two small circles where the judges wanted the popper birds and shot fliers to fall. Confined falls would help late-running dogs from becoming confused by a maze of scent from scattered birds.

To a retriever trained first to fetch plastic dummies, then dead pigeons, flying pigeons, and finally flying ducks and pheasants, there is a palpable difference between plastic and bird. As for the choice between dead meat and a big cackling pheasant breaking the skyline in accelerating flight, it is no choice at all. Retrievers ache for the flier. They check to see which gun team has the crates of live birds and which is faking it with sacks of dead poppers. Among multiple birds, retrievers will usually go for the last one down. In this test, the judges decided that the flier would be the last bird down and the first one retrieved, making the popper the "memory bird," challenging the dog's ability to remember the earlier mark.

Bath turned to the trial committee and offered them an opportunity for comment on the test. "Listen," he said, "if we're crapping in our mess kits, let us know now. We'll listen."

Retriever trials used to be based on hunting, testing above all the retriever's most valuable function: finding wounded birds. A pheasant with a broken wing but good legs still beneath it is an evasive sprinter, fast enough to challenge any retriever in shape. The British bred their Labs and Goldens to track and catch these runners, and their field trials, which are essentially hunts, still test the dogs on those birds by pass shooting from butts (blinds) and "walking up" pheasants before an advancing line. In British trials, if one retriever has the good fortune of being sent for a pheasant flushed from under his nose and dropped close by, and another dog has to run down an unseen cripple for a half mile through The Bog From Hell, so be it—that's the fortuitous nature of hunting.

The crippled bird and natural hunting conditions are still in the AKC rule book but no longer in the trials. Crippled fliers, though rare at a National, get "No bird!" from the judges, and the dog is pulled from the line to run at a later time. The line at field trials is static; it does not proceed as it once did across a field, flushing birds before the moving guns and dogs. Retriever field trials in this country resemble neither hunting nor much else. They are a competitive game of their own.

The judges make the tests increasingly more diffi-cult—"artificial" is the word heard most at these trials—because the retrievers keep pushing the envelope, and judges have to work down huge fields of dogs to a man-ageable number. Trainers of the old school are of the opinion that trial judges today are less interested in seeing what a dog can do than what a dog can't do.

"You try to play on the dog's strengths and cover his weaknesses," Sweezey says. "The judges are just the opposite. They're trying to uncover weaknesses."

To test their ability not to switch, judges for a time were putting "over and unders" in vogue—two marks, one short, one longer, dropped in a line. From the dog's perspective the birds appear to land together. Judges also do pinchers, two marks thrown at each other to fall close together. "Tight" marks tempt switching. When the dog is about to go for a mark, judges might add a "wipeout" bird, a flier shot close to the sitting dog and on an arc over the course he will have to maintain to the more distant one—if he now can remember it. Wipeout birds erase memory birds and tempt non-slip retrievers to slip. So do "fly-aways," fliers purposely missed by the gunners and allowed to fly out of sight. When pheasants reached ten bucks a bird, fly-aways flew away from field trials altogether.

The most diabolical variation of all is to require that the dog run past a "poison bird," a mark he is forbidden to retrieve. On a retriever's scale of passions denied, poison birds are right up there with garden hose coitus interruptus.

As the week of the National progressed, the tests would increase in complexity and distractions—triple marks, quad marks, fliers as memory birds, multiple fliers, guns that retired (hid) after firing, dry pops (shooting, but no birds thrown), rougher ground, deeper falls. Bath and Company did not include wipeouts, fly-aways, or poison birds, but the first tests would be no picnic.

When I asked Dennis Bath what he hoped to accomplish with the first test, he said, "We just want to *finish* the first test on Monday. You worry about splitting it."

Insofar as possible—and it rarely is—the judges want each test to throw up equal obstacles for all the dogs. But as this was the largest number of dogs yet to run in a National Championship Stake and it often rains on the second day of the National, they worried that a split test would push some of the eighty-five dogs into a wet disadvantage. There would be grumbling around the trucks. The American obsession with competition dominates these trials.

All this has led to a movement in recent years for less demanding retriever tests that better approximate the conditions of hunting. The AKC licenses such hunting tests, which evaluate the dogs on five different abilities, rather than in competition against each other for a blue ribbon. "You have to be careful when you're talking to a dyed-in-the-wool field trialer," said Ham Rowan, "because they think hunting tests are for failed field trialers. Give it five or ten years and there will be more hunting tests than field trials, because it's only a few who have the money, time, and competitive bent to run in field trials. A lot of hunters don't want to put their retrievers through the stress of all that training. To make a Lab competitive for field trials, you have to be out there with the dog every day. Who has that time? You have to hire a pro. But who has that kind of money? The rule book says they're supposed to be judging in a hunting context, but you don't go hunting in a white coat. Hunting tests aren't more for the average guy, they *are* for the average guy. But when you have a Master Hunter title on your dog, you have a super dog. By god, you don't have 'no birds' in our hunting tests. You're sent on that pheasant with the one dangling leg, and you'd better track that bird. That's why the British trialers, who hunt cripples, cannot understand our American field trials. This 'no bird' stuff is nonsense, but not from the field trialers' standpoint—they want everything equal because they are in competition. Our field trials are admittedly not hunting. It's a game, the difference between hardball and softball. I'm not pooh-poohing field trials. Field trials are hardball."

Hunters, however, still follow their curiosities to field trials, watch the polished talent, and conclude, "I sure would like to have a dog that does those things."

Dennis Bath called for a "setup" dog to run retrieves on the birds. Setup dogs would help reveal obstacles—and inequities—the judges couldn't see and confirm what they could: confusing angles on multiple birds, a blinding glare off a pond, a depression putting the dogs running blind retrieves too long out of sight of their handlers, and any number of problems that could make what was intended to be a competitive test a contentious one.

The setup dog disappeared into the eroded depressions and came up far right of the flier.

"That's dead dog canyon out there," Snow said.

The wind was at the judges' backs. They set up the tests downwind, because dogs running (and particularly swimming) upwind to a deep blind can't hear their handlers' whistles. The judges then walked across the gullies, looked back, and set up the same test in reverse. In the event the wind shifted one hundred eighty degrees on the day of the trial, they would be prepared to "flip" the test.

They ran more setup dogs, checking their stop watches as each dog returned with the bird. Seven minutes. Eighty-five retrievers in the first series of competition.

"Almost ten hours," said Snow. "That's all the daylight we have—if everything goes perfectly, which of course it won't. I like the look of the terrain. It's a pretty spot. You don't want to bring people here from all over the country and show them junked cars. The National is a nice combination of show and go."

"The first dog is show."

"You want something for the gallery that first day."

"I'd like a rooster on that first flier, wouldn't you, Clint?"

"Yes, a nice big cock pheasant against that sky would be pretty."

"Those dogs won't need anything to pump them up more than they're already pumped. But a cock bird would be a good idea."

That night the bird steward informed the judges of a shortage of roosters. The first flier would be a hen.

Doors were slamming and aluminum lawn chairs screeching open in the gallery as darkness gradually drained from the eastern sky. It was 45 degrees, cool enough for a turtleneck and sweatshirt. Loudspeakers were strapped to the roof of a pickup truck. Through a squeal of feedback came an announcement that all handlers who wanted to watch the "test dogs" were invited to the line. The test dogs—two for each test—would allow the competing handlers to size up the obstacles under a non-competing retriever.

The handlers worry about the light and can do nothing about it. The early dogs running before dawn and the late ones at dusk have trouble seeing their marks in the gloom, or the sun may be in their eyes. God willing, it will be at their backs, lighting up the bird like a Fokker over London.

But of all the obstacles, the one that causes handlers to toss in their beds is the wind. At trials, Sweezey will on occasion meet the test dog returning with a duck, pluck some feathers, hold them high, and watch the drift. Retrievers don't like to cast into the wind. Yet they are judged on how straight a line they maintain to the birds, despite their tendency to drift with the wind, despite the distraction of other scent and rough cover, despite their instinct to go out there and simply hunt, quartering left and right, circling, running, charging their batteries.

"I've seen Nationals lost when the wind changes," Sweezey said. "Dogs will fade with the wind. It takes a really tough dog to stay straight on a line. Casting a dog into the wind is the toughest thing. Dogs want to quarter. If you get a dog running the last deep bird of a triple with a crosswind from the left, you can't send him straight or he'll fade off to that last bird on the right he just retrieved. That's 'returning to a fall'—a penalty. So you false cast him to the left of the true line, and he'll fade with the wind over to the bird."

A crowd of men and women in white coats, small whistles on lanyards dangling from their necks, walked down toward the line. Sweezey, towering above them, was in the lead, his whistle—a shrill, pealess Fox 40—bouncing against his sternum. Like Sweezey, most of them were pros, in the business of training and handling their clients' dogs. In forty-seven years of National Championship Stakes, amateurs had won only fifteen. The pros had dominated—Charles Morgan, Cotton Pershall, Billy Wunderlich, Roy Gonia, Joe Riser, D. L. Walters, Bach Doar, Tommy Sorenson.

Four of the amateur wins had been by Paul Bakewell III of St. Louis (1942, 1943, 1946, and 1949), three with the same dog, Shed of Arden. Shed was out of a litter named for fish. Shed was a misspelled shad. Cotton Pershall trained Shed and the rest of Bakewell's dogs (and later those of John M. Olin at Nilo Farms). Having advised

Bakewell that the dogs could see his arm signals better if he wore white, Cotton takes responsibility for introducing white coats to field trials. At the 1956 National in Weldon Springs, Missouri, Bakewell looked out at the first test and turned to Cotton.

"What are all those people in the field doing wearing white coats?"

"That's to make it equal so all the dogs can see the guns."

"They aren't supposed to mark those coats, they're supposed to mark the birds."

For nearly twenty years following Bakewell, the amateurs were virtually shut out at the winner's table. Then August Belmont, scion of the Belmont Stakes, showed up at the 1968 National with his brainy Lab Super Chief. Augie Belmont had won two previous National Amateurs with Soupy, and they hammered the 1968 National. Both Soupy and Belmont were trained by Rex Carr in the San Joaquin Valley of California. Carr had revolutionized retriever training with the electronic collar, training the dog and his owner as a team. The amateurs, many of them out of the West Coast and Carr trained, began clobbering the pros in field trials. And they began winning the Nationals: Creole Sister, Royal's Moose's Moe, Wanapum Dart's Dandy, San Joaquin Honcho, Euroclydon, Shadow of Otter Creek, Risky Business Ruby, Orion's Sky, Wanapum's Lucyana Girl. The pros got edgy. They weren't all that pleased about Carr training amateurs to beat them. And their clients, occupying the front chairs in the gallery, straightened their Loden capes and concluded that the neighborhood was going to hell in bluejeans.

The AKC rules require that all field trial judges be amateurs, and for the National—which shifts each year to a different time zone—that they reside in time zones outside the locus of the National. Dennis Bath owned an office supply and furniture store in Belleville, Illinois. Tony Snow was a software engineer for U.S. West in Seattle. Clint Joyner taught history at a high school in Smithfield, North Carolina. All were experienced trialers and judges, amateurs only in fine print.

"The judges this year are as good as they come."

"Tony and Dennis are excellent test setters. You can't say that too often about judges."

"Dennis is not going to let a dog win who tippy-toes into the water."

The handlers reached the line—a runner of green indoor-outdoor carpet—and formed a loose crescent around the judges. Bath turned toward the gallery. His gold bracelet and Rolex were visible, as they were meant to be, even in the dim light. Ring, necklace, bracelet, watch—he was happily burdened by the troy ounce; the trialers called him Jingles. In his red turtleneck, gray sweater, and moleskin trousers, Bath was what Sweezey would describe as "a natty dresser," but he was all dog business. Bath had won both the 1979 and 1980 National Amateur Championship Stakes with his black Lab Lawhorn's Cadillac Mack.

"All right," he yelled, motioning over the heads of the handlers, "let's have the first test dog!"

A man walked out and stood on the pad with his yellow Lab off leash and at heel. James Parker, real estate, Austin, Texas. The Lab sat at his left side, tense, alert, looking out where the meadow dropped away into the braids of the wash and then rose to the horizon a half mile away. Rough, choppy range, cluttered with brush and occasional scrub trees. Dead Dog Canyon.

Bath waved his clipboard over his head and shouted, "Guns up!"

In the distance, the white coats rose from their chairs. The Lab swung her head from gun team to gun team, getting a picture of their positions, the tableau, anticipating the birds. Her name was FC-AFC Powder It White. She had "earned her initials": Field Champion (FC) and Amateur Field Champion (AFC). Field trials licensed by the American Kennel Club award championship points in major stakes—five points for a win, three for second place, one for third, half a point for fourth. A retriever gets its FC (and AFC when handled by an amateur) after accumulating ten points, which must include a win. Winning a trial against a large field of highly trained retrievers does not come easily. To qualify for the National, a retriever has to earn seven points, including a win, all in the twelve months since the last National. Powder was one point shy.

But she had run in many trials and seen numerous birds. She understood the game.

Behind his back, Parker signalled to the judges that Powder was ready. Bath waved his clipboard slowly over his head, signalling the guns. On the rise above the pond, the popper guns fired as a dead pheasant tumbled through the air. Powder quivered, her head snapping toward the second team. She saw the crates. Come on, gimme the flier. Bath raised the clipboard again. From the near guns, a live pheasant was thrown into the air. Gaining altitude, it roared away, a momentary silhouette against the dull dawn sky before abruptly folding and falling away from a puff of feathers that hung in the air. The collective boom of the shotguns reached the gallery.

"Test dog," Bath announced, the signal to Parker that he was now free to send his dog.

Powder had her butt on the mat. Her eyes were fixed on where the flier had gone down. She was steady. She did not creep, did not break. A non-slip retriever.

Parker said, "Powder!" and the dog exploded into a run, slashed downhill through the high grass, and disappeared.

The handlers were attentive. The gulch would put their dogs not only momentarily out of sight of their marks but also out of the competition if they blew too far off course. To maintain a straight retrieve to the memory bird, the dogs would have to cross some ridges, go up a cut bank, and swim across the end of the upper pond. The nature of dogs is to prefer land rather than water to get to their prey, to run the bank rather than swim. In field trials, bank running is a minor fault. (To hunters, it is nothing of the sort if it gets their dog on the bird more quickly, especially a lightly hit pheasant with cross-country ambitions or a duck floating downriver on a fast current. Field trialers argue that a straight running or swimming retriever will more accurately find his mark and get less disoriented when going through cover.) Some hunting by the dog in the vicinity of the fall is expected, but judges will penalize a long hunt as proof that the dog did not accurately mark the fall. Field trials are tests—over formidable distances and demoniac obstacles—of the confluence of retriever genes and endless training.

Powder came out of the wash on a line to the fallen flier. She beat around in the high brush and saplings—"putting on a little hunt," as Parker said—then stopped, her tail up, her head down. She ran back across the gully holding the warm pheasant in her mouth. She trotted up the hill, tail wagging, pivoted by Parker's left leg, and sat at heel. He reached over her head and removed the dead bird. Powder tongued wet feathers from her mouth, never taking her eyes off the popper team. Without taking his eyes off Powder, Parker held the bird out behind him. Bath stood up from his chair to receive the handoff, and passed it to one of the game stewards. The pheasant dropped into a bag. The flier was now a popper.

Parker leaned forward, extending his left hand above the bridge of Powder's nose in the direction of the fallen popper, "giving the dog the line." Cocking the dog. Steadying the dog.

He spoke her name. She was off. She "stepped on" the popper. Powder It White returned to applause from the gallery.

She would now run the blind retrieve. Before Parker had brought Powder to the line, a bird boy had come over the horizon, placed a dead pheasant in front of a bush, and had run back over the hill out of sight. The handlers watched all this so that they could direct their dogs. But the dogs would be in ignorance of the bird's location, running blind. During the setups the previous week, the gun teams had used pieces of orange tape to identify their positions and the places for the falls. Tony Snow had rejected ribbons for the blind bird and asked the grounds crew to drag a tree limb to it. "I don't like all those ribbons out there," Snow had said. "I like to see the blind marked as naturally as possible. When I'm duck hunting, I don't see many orange ribbons marking my falls."

Powder would be running blind for three hundred yards, crossing the tail of the wash and a deep swale that would drop her momentarily out of sight of Parker. Her departure was critical.

"You like their nose to tail lined up," Sweezey said. "But they'll go where they're looking. A dog looks right down his nose. You see which way that nose is pointing— that's where the dog will go."

Blind tests determine how well a retriever runs under the handler's control—taking the initial line, stopping and sitting at a whistle blast, casting in the direction of arm signals—while maintaining a direct course to the unseen bird. The ideal is for the dog to "line the blind," running hundreds of yards without a whistle or cast straight to the bird.

This blind had an additional obstacle: the dogs would have to go behind the flier guns. Guns always stand facing the fall of their bird. Field trial retrievers are trained not to run behind the guns and are penalized if they do, unless that is the only direct route to another bird. Artificial to a fault, this test would demand tight control over the dogs, which could be pushed off course by the presence of the guns.

Parker cocked his hand over Powder. He said, "Back!" and out she went. The guns did not push her off course, but Parker had misjudged the location of the blind and Powder overran the bird. Parker blew his whistle; she sat; he pointed down and whistled—beep, beep, beep, beep—the come-in command. She came in and got the bird.

Parker concluded that they had run "a not so good blind."

The sun appeared at the horizon, and a light breeze bent the bluestem. After a second test dog ran the test, the loudspeakers announced, "FC-AFC Honcho's Sundance to the line." The National was under way.

Jay Sweezey stood in the grass behind the gallery, leaning over his truck, watching the dogs compete. He would be running two black Labs owned by the Atterburys: Hawkeye's Smokey Joe, a male, and B. B. Powder, a bitch. Smokey was the nineteenth dog to run that morning, B. B. fifty-sixth. Sweezey was pleased he hadn't pulled an early number. He was content to let other dogs stumble over and disclose the problems out there before he cocked his dogs.

Risky Business Jem was heading for the gully in high gear. Her mother, Risky Business Ruby, had won the 1980 National. "Roswell, New Mexico," Sweezey said, his eyes still on the dog. "I was there." As Jem began swinging wide of the fall, Sweezey lowered his voice.

"Easy, girl, easy now."

Rick Roberts walked up to Sweezey. They were nearly neighbors on the Eastern Shore and good friends, despite their differences in age (Rick is forty-nine) and training. Rick is a pro of the new school. Sweezey says that Rick is one of the few handlers he can talk to about something other than dogs.

"What've we got here, Jay?"

"We've got a double mark and a blind."

"Is the blind under the flier?"

"No, behind the guns. Jem just lined the blind."

They chatted briefly about the test, then Sweezey walked back to his truck to get Smokey. Rick stayed to evaluate the competition.

Rick was wearing what he always wears when training and at trials—a white, long-sleeved, buttoned-down oxford cloth shirt and Levis. A cobbler in Maine had made his mocassins. Except for ovals of white around his eyes, Rick's round face was darkly tanned. When the sun rose higher he would put on his aviator sunglasses, which he is rarely without. His advice to people looking for a retriever trainer is don't trust a pro who isn't tan. Unlike Sweezey, he hates hats. His gray hair begins late on his brow and is combed straight back. He grew up in Bethesda, Maryland, a suburb of Washington, D.C., and in his boyhood the nearest he got to the outdoors was the woods along Massachusetts Avenue extended, well beyond the embassies. "I was a typical suburban kid."

"My mother had a phobia about dogs," he said. "She was really frightened of them; consequently we never had any. I always wanted a dog."

Rick studied at Washington and Lee, then halfway into law school at American University decided that he wasn't interested in following his father into the practice of law. After passing the D.C. bar examination, he taught English and history for ten years, off and on, in the Fairfax County schools of Virginia.

"I would have quit sooner had it been a city school. I like the country. I like to hunt and fish."

For his first dog Rick bought a Labrador, but it was from show ring breeding and wouldn't retrieve. He then bought Beaver, a two-year-old Lab trained, in a charitable manner of speaking, as a gun dog. Beaver's approach to retrieving was one of diminishing returns. As Rick and his hunting companion waded around the marshes of Assateague putting out decoys, Beaver was busy returning them to the shore.

"In 1969, the National was in Smyrna, Delaware, so I went over and watched a few series. I said to myself that I would sure like to have a dog that could do those things."

Rick wanted a hand in training his dog and running it in all the stakes—something the old school did not encourage. That led him to California, where he studied under Rex Carr, learning to be a "collar" trainer. Rick ran his first field trial in 1978. Five years later he and his wife, Patti, turned pro. Patti teaches the young dogs the basics—sit, heel, here, back, over, no, *no!* Rick does the polishing. Beaver Dam Kennels, Trappe, Maryland—twenty-four indoor/outdoor runs. Managing a kennel and training dogs is like running a dairy: no days off. Patti was home with the dogs.

Rick is a sympathetic observer who brings body English and some of the emphatic spoken word to the gallery when he watches other dogs run. He stood with his hands thrust into his back pockets as Hugh Arthur, a pro from Georgia, sent Razzy for the flier. Arthur had won the 1985 National.

"This is the time when you really die," Rick said, "standing up there on the line just *waiting* for your dog to come up with the bird."

Razzy was getting confused in the eroded hummocks. "Hey, this flier could be trouble. Man, this is a . . . *Ooooooh!*" Rick turned away, visibly pained, as the Lab disappeared. He wanted to win the National, but he got little satisfaction seeing another dog in trouble.

Razzy had what Rick called a "hellaciously long hunt" on the flier and some difficulty finding the popper.

"Generally, the judges allow you two mistakes," he said. "That could be whistles, that is, having to handle on a mark, a big no-no. When you get a dog like this that has had to hunt long for the flier and had a bad mark on the memory bird, some judges would drop that dog now. But this is the National, and it's taken these people incredible competition to get here. Good judges like Dennis Bath and Tony Snow will try to let most of the dogs go through at least two series before starting to drop them."

Razzy was on his way back from the blind with the bird when he staggered and lay down in the grass. Hugh Arthur broke from the line and hurried down the hill. He returned, carrying the dog prostrate in his arms. Suspecting heat exhaustion, one of the veterinarian trialers shouted for ice. Coolers came out of the trucks. Razzy was quickly buried under a mound of ice cubes.

Field trial retrievers are high-spirited dogs. They spend much of their time on the truck, waiting in dark confinement, hearing the guns, the whistles, the loudspeaker—trial sounds. When they come out to work, they are cranked up like cheetahs stalking a gazelle. The insufferable wait behind three successive holding blinds—the field trial equivalent of on-deck circles—cranks them even higher. Then come the blistering runs, and in Razzy's case a long hunt in heavy, humid cover.

Arthur said that it wasn't heat exhaustion, that Razzy had done this before in the cold of winter. "He did this more when he was young. Some say it's low blood sugar, but that's not the case. The vets aren't sure what his problem is. If he gets overexcited, he'll fall out on you once in a while. I sensed he was in trouble coming out of the holding blind. His hind legs were getting a little wobbly."

Eventually a rectal thermometer showed that Razzy's temperature had dropped to one hundred and four and was on its way to normal. The dog stood up, shook himself, and wagged his tail. He was remarkably frisky, but he had booted the first series. Razzy would not be among the call-backs posted that night at the Holiday Inn in Duncan.

The odds of winning a field trial, much less the National, do not attract serious gamblers to the sport. "In any trial, you can have fifty to eighty retrievers, even more," said Sweezey. "Only one can win. Those are pretty tough odds. How many times have you bet a horse race at eighty to one?"

The remote odds at this National seemed to favor a black Labrador named Trumarc's Zip Code. Cody was owned and trained by Judy Aycock, considered to be the most successful amateur, if not the best handler period, on the circuit. Judy won the 1976 National with Cody's father, San Joaquin Honcho, and the 1984 National

Amateur with Cody, and is often a finalist. At eleven years of age, his muzzle as gray as ash, Cody had enough ribbons on his chest and hash marks on his sleeve to command a fleet. He had accumulated more championship points than any other dog at this National and had the second highest total in the history of the game.

"But the odds of his winning the National aren't like the odds of Sugar Ray Leonard beating that Canadian," Rick Roberts said. "The National winner is usually a very good dog, but this is not like horses, which pretty much run the same time, depending on the track. Dennis Bath won the National Amateur in Maine with Cadillac Mack, and that fall we went to Roswell, New Mexico, for the National Championship and Mack went out in the first series. Just because you have a good dog doesn't mean he'll win the National."

Sweezey and Smokey were in the last of the three holding blinds. Sitting in a folding chair behind a low screen of canvas stretched taut between iron stakes, Sweezey could observe up close the play in the field. Smokey could not, but he had no trouble having his amperage further goosed by the sounds of the action.

Sweezey leaned forward, his outstretched arm resting on a stake. He was intent on watching Judy Aycock and Cody go to the line. Some dogs have trouble thinking on their feet, Rick said, but Cody is cerebral. "Cody just doesn't go out there and be stupid."

Cody had passed on his smarts. He was competing against eight of his own progeny at this National. He may have been an old dog, but if necessary, he could still swim out of sight for a duck. Cody sat slowly.

Bench people would not say that Cody was a beautiful Lab. He was far from the line of stout Labs favored in the show ring: not blocky, not otter-tailed. Cody was lean, rather long in the snout, rangy—an American field trial retriever.

In this country, both Labrador and Golden Retriever blood has diverged and gone into two separate pools, producing two different lines of dogs: those for show and those for field trial. In the debate over what is the proper dog—a beauty or a retriever—plates can fly.

"Some of these field trial dogs are downright ugly. But they can do the job."

"I've told them to their faces, and they're good friends, that their Labs don't even look like Labs. They've got long, pointy noses."

"That Honcho dog was absolutely the worst-looking Lab I've ever seen. He looked like a whippet."

"Show dogs have been bred away from their origins simply to meet a standard of conformation. They lack drive, don't mark or retrieve."

"Show people want their Labs to have barrelly-looking bodies and big heads. I think if any field trialer sees show blood in the pedigree, he won't even consider the dog."

"You used to see dual champions, both show and field. It's damned rare nowadays."

"The field trial people have gone to leggier, faster running Labs. The show Labs don't look like the show Labs used to look—they're dumpier. I wish we could get both groups going toward the middle, so we could again have a dual champion."

Judy sent Cody for the flier. He drove straight to the pheasant, returned with it comfortably in his mouth, then went out and nailed the memory bird. Cody had hammered his marks. Judy lined him up for the blind retrieve, slightly bending her knees, extending her hand.

"Back!"

He went. She whistled him to a sit and recast him four times before he reached the bird. But Cody did not vary more than ten or fifteen degrees off each cast. It was a decent blind. Cody would be on the call-back list.

Sweezey rose from his chair and removed Smokey's chain collar and short lead. The snaps and ring were solid brass from a harnessmaker in Lexington. The loudspeaker announced FC-AFC-CFC Hawkeye's Smokey Joe (he had also won his initials in Canada).

Sweezey walked forward to the line. In trials, he often loosens up the judges with something ribald as his dog is returning from a long retrieve, but at the National he saved his jokes for the gallery. Sweezey was concerned about Smokey.

"He's not a National type dog," he had said, "he's a six- or seven-series dog." Smokey was hyper in the truck, and his steam often clouded his better judgment. Sweezey sometimes had trouble "checking him down," getting him to hunt short instead of driving past the birds.

"A National kind of dog," Sweezey says, "is level-headed and watches his birds very intensely. A dog can have a mediocre blind, but has to be on his marks. You can have journeymen blinds, but get nines and tens on marks and you'll be there in the end."

With his cupped left hand, Sweezey lightly tapped his thigh to draw Smokey's haunches into line.

The guns fired. Dennis Bath said, "Number nineteen," and Sweezey sent the dog. Smokey had little trouble finding the flier, but his recollection of the memory bird had dissipated. He failed to check down. He overran the bird, hunting the hill above and behind the guns. Smokey improved on the blind, but when Sweezey passed by on his way back to the truck, he was not in a celebratory mood. Smokey would survive the call-backs, but he was using up his chits.

Observing all this from the third holding blind was Dottie Metcalf, a wiry woman with snow-white hair, comfortably past middle-age. Secretary of the National Amateur Retriever Club, she had run her Labs in previous Nationals and numerous National Amateurs, but the experience had not lightened the stress. A week before the National, she had arrived in Ardmore, Oklahoma, with Rick Roberts and the dogs to train with the Aycocks and another friend for this championship. She was accustomed to training and trialing in the East, where walls of trees drew in the horizon. She had looked out at Oklahoma and was in awe of the distances.

Dottie Metcalf and her late husband, Dick, had bought their first Labrador shortly after they were married, and with some attention to their copy of James Lamb Free's *Training Your Retriever* they began entering retriever field trials. "Dickie ran the dog—I threw. I was the bird boy." His temperament was not suited to dog training and trials, however, and in a few years he gave it up.

Dave Elliot, the Scottish trainer, who was some years beyond Wingan Kennel and the employ of Jay Carlisle, was running a high-class boarding kennel in New Jersey, where he helped teach Dottie how to run retrievers. Elliot had introduced the whistle and handling commands to American retriever field trials, but in the years before his death in 1985 he had come to regret what he considered the excessive use in trials of the whistle, of over-control. He wanted to see retrievers think on their feet.

Dottie enjoyed the competition of field trials (she had put some Labs with Sweezey), but she was then also occupied with golf, fox hunting, and time on the road with a son who had developed into a competitive figure skater. When Dick sold his auto dealership in Asbury Park, the Metcalfs moved from New Jersey to Oxford, on Maryland's Eastern Shore.

"When we moved there," Dottie had told me, "Dickie got a sailboat. I thought sailing was for the birds. He was not a joiner, and the only people I knew were dog people, so I got more involved in field trials. Dickie's family had steeplechasers and a plantation in South Carolina. They were an outdoor family, unlike mine. After we were married, I was invited duck hunting a few times and I liked that."

Dottie met Patti and Rick Roberts, who lived nearby. They helped train her dogs—and helped train her. They often work dogs together on the Metcalfs' farm, with a circle of other Roberts clients who share the duties of throwing marks, popping, and setting blinds. Patti shoots the fliers. (Sweezey hires an assistant and trains alone.)

Sitting beside Dottie in the holding blind was her pride and nemesis, Pot Pie's W. A. Megan. Megan was a compact, low-slung black Labrador bitch that could be a retrieving machine and, at times, something of a royal pain. The W. A. in her name stood for Wild Ass.

"Megan has so much desire," Rick said, "an all-out, unbelievable desire for the birds regardless of the terrain or the training pressures." He and Patti had raised Megan, as they had Riggo—another Metcalf dog that Rick would run—before selling them to Dottie.

"Both Megan and Riggo are pretty happy-go-lucky," Rick said. "Neither holds a grudge. Riggo is much more willing to please, more aware that someone is in control. Megan is far more willful. She wants to have her own way. She's a really talented dog, but she is not as sensitive to training and doesn't retain it as well as Riggo does. But she has one saving grace—she's so lovable and cute. If she were at all unattractive, she would have been shot by now." Dottie did not disagree.

Megan was eight years old, nearing the age when many field trial dogs hang it up and lie by the andirons. She was good-looking as field trial Labs go, was certainly no plump suburban groaner. Her shoulder muscles were granitic. As with any professional athlete, however, the heavy schedule of competition and training had worn her down. Megan had required knee surgery for torn cruciate ligaments, and her hips were bad. Many big dogs, retrievers among them, have dysplastic, or malformed, hip sockets. The Orthopedic Foundation for Animals at the University of Missouri reviews hip X-rays of dogs and records the degree of hip joint conformation in a Dysplasia Control Registry. The dog's owner receives a certificate that rates the hips from excellent on down into dysplastic territory.

Megan's were so dysplastic that the OFA refused to register her, and Dottie would not breed her.

Riggo was a rugged, thick-coated black Lab with all the optimism of any sophomore. "Riggo is a National-caliber dog," Rick said, "but I don't really expect him to win here. He's just turning four. When Riggo qualified for this National, he was ahead of my schedule for him."

Dottie keeps Megan in the house and Riggo in an outdoor run. "Except for the cocktail hour," she said, "then I let him indoors. Only when Rick and Patti go south for their winter training will my dogs be away from me. And then in January I go down there with them."

Dottie and Megan were at the line. The guns fired. As Megan bounded into the wash, Rick, standing behind the gallery, could see that she was bearing wide of the line to the flier. She came out of the wash flying but in dangerous territory well away from the bird. His folded arms tightened.

"Come on, hon," he said, "get over there. That scent's not so good."

Megan hunted long and aggressively in the brush for the flier, quartering, subdividing the cover, whirling to charge down the hill, then turning and running back up, ransacking the hillside.

Rick was in agony, rocking on his heels. "Ah . . aahhhhh . . *Jeeeeeeez!* It's right *in* there!" Megan finally stopped, only her whipping tail visible above the grass, and picked up the dead pheasant.

Rick did not relax. "The longer they hunt, the easier it is to forget that memory bird."

Megan came up with the memory bird.

On the blind retrieve, about a hundred yards out, Megan disappeared into a swale. She did not come out. Dogs get anxious on long blinds. They don't know where they are going. The worriers just "pop"—stop and check back. Minor fault. Dottie was also afraid that Megan might be hunting. Blinds are not meant to test hunting abilities; they are strictly obedience tests. Megan had to keep driving and not hunt. Where in blazes was she? Dottie cupped her hands around the whistle and blew. Megan bounced up in view and sat. She was left of plumb.

Dottie's cast would have to account for Megan's windward drift over a long run through stuff that could make hash of a straight line. Megan had been trained, as most trial retrievers are, to spin on a back-cast in the direction of the arm raised—a right arm up gets a left spin back, a left arm a right spin. The dog's momentum tends to carry it back in the direction of the spin. Megan sat in the grass looking back at Dottie. Standing with her legs apart, Dottie threw her right arm up at one o'clock, an "angle back" more back than over—what Sweezey calls a bover.

"Back!" she shouted. Rick groaned again.

"Ooooh, come on, Dottie," he said quietly, "Walk it out, let her see you."

Rick wanted Dottie to step forcefully to the right so that Megan, at that distance, would not mistake the cast.

Megan did not mistake the cast. She spun and charged back, her momentum on the turn carrying her slightly right on a long parabola that soon had her again drifting left with the wind away from the blind. After a few more casts, Megan got to the pheasant.

"This isn't how you want to start the first series at the National," Rick said, as Dottie walked Megan back to her van. "You want to get through the first three or four series without any problem. I don't mean that you have to stomp them. But you don't want to have a lot of mistakes early, because the judges won't allow you any more."

It was now evident that all eighty-five retrievers could not be run through this series in the first day, pushing Riggo—number eighty-five—into the following day. A split test. Rick was ambivalent. In yesterday's training, Riggo had gotten "all screwed up" in a ravine looking for a bird, and Rick had had to recast him a number of times.

"He was really pooped and confused, but we shot him a number of fliers to get him back up. Maybe having a day off will help him. Maybe not. The National is always a crapshoot. A big front is coming in from the west, and tomorrow it will be blowing fifty miles an hour. If it's in your face, the dog can't hear the whistle on blinds."

When Dottie returned, Rick said, "I just couldn't believe she couldn't come up with that flier!"

"I think she smelled something going over," Dottie said. "Then she was so tired after that long hunt for the flier, when I tried to line her on the blind her head was up panting rather than looking out where I wanted her to. We should have trained last week with chairs in the holding blinds. Riggo's going to hop in your lap when he gets there."

Dottie was hungry. She walked over to the snack trailer and bought a cup of coffee and a cinnamon roll. I bought two strips of peppered beef jerky. It was good jerky, of riding crop prime, but I had eaten breakfast well before dawn, and I rushed the jerky. I nearly yanked out my teeth.

"For someone not running a dog," Dottie said, "a trial can be boring." She walked back to the van to get a chair and her needlework.

The guns live well. There were eighteen in all, mostly retired—a dentist, a cop, an insurance man, a sugar distributor, a Harvard MBA, a mechanic, a Pan Am pilot, a banker—an intermittent fraternity of traveling men who enjoy each other's company, wing shooting, the traditions of the guns, ample food, and the fluid comforts of the Doobissary.

The Doobissary is a thirty-two-foot Travco RV with an orange stripe down its side.

For fifteen years of Nationals and National Amateurs, the Doobissary has served as the bar, restaurant, and resting spa of the official guns, each of whom antes up twenty or thirty dollars to pay for the food, drinks, and gas. For years the man who kept the till and purchased the provisions was a California gun known as Dooby. Dooby was of the school of accounting that rounded some distance from the nearest decimal, handing down a tradition that entitles the gun who manages the buying to keep the unspent twenty or so. This is formalized at the conclusion of the trial when the guns, en bloc, announce approval of the account as "accurate to the penny."

Clive Ostenburg, captain of the guns for this National, had held a meeting of the guns the previous evening in his motel room in Duncan. One might more accurately describe it as a brief intermission between the hot dip and bourbon. He had concluded business in a few minutes.

"The judges have asked us to remain standing after firing until the dog picks up the bird," he had said. There had been theatrical groaning from confirmed sitters. "For the poppers, it will be shoot, throw, shoot. On the fliers, the guns are to ride them out. I'm thirsty."

Ostenberg was a taciturn man, a banker from Scotts-bluff, Nebraska, who ran a farm and flew gliders and acrobatic planes. "This is probably my fiftieth National, if you include the National Amateurs. These guys have been shooting together for probably thirty years."

From years of shooting, many of the guns were hard of hearing. They ribbed each other in loud voices.

"What's that, Clive?"

"I can't hear you."

"What'd he say, Ted?"

"What?"

"*What?*"

The tradition of official guns, which was well under way in the early 1930s, developed something approaching formality in the winter of 1939 when Ernest Burton wrote to Percy Cushing to suggest the organization of a gunners' union. The letter traveled from Fifth Avenue to Broadway. Burton envisioned three grades of gunners. The first grade would be a limited number of Boomers, qualified to shoot "at any trial under any circumstances. That is all that can usually hit anything anyway." Poppers could only shoot when accompanied by a Boomer. The last grade would be Squibs. Squibs would carry shells and make drinks for the Boomers. Squibs were the wives. Burton suggested Cushing as president, "the Big Noise," and for vice president, Bill Harder of Lincoln, Nebraska, by most accounts the best wing shot in the country. (Harder would later introduce Clive Ostenberg to the club.)

Burton did not believe in elaborate organizations. "Since dues involve money, and money involves debts, and debts are a very unhappy thing, the simplest way to eliminate all this unhappiness is to eliminate the Treasurer." His by-laws were brief: a gunner must never shoot a dog, a fellow gun, or a judge. "There is no penalty for shooting the gallery, but this is strongly recommended against, as the cost comes high. . . . Guns shall remain sufficiently sober during the time of the trial to be able to answer truthfully in the affirmitive to the club's password." The password cum motto was, "Can you hit your hat?"

Burton was serious, however, about the routines he helped establish for gunning at retriever trials. A gun who ignored a rule was not invited back. Anything but double shotguns (over-and-unders or side-by-sides) was frowned upon. The guns do not want to wonder if some invited shooter has unloaded. They want to see that open gun, broken at the breech, daylight down the tubes. They do not close their shotguns until the dog is brought to the line.

The gun pins are enamel and display a deerstalker's cap above a blunderbuss: blue pins for squibs, green for poppers, red for boomers. Gun captains are not liberal with their pins. A gun has to pop at trials for five or six years before he gets the green. To make the boomer circle, he may have to shoot for another six, maybe more; when finally initiated, he has to throw up his hat and shoot it.

Clive Ostenberg, who had been sitting in the sun on the bumper of the Doobissary, rose to go back inside. "In the nineteen-fifties and early sixties," he said, "we had General Curtis LeMay, Fes Parker, and Andy Devine as gunners. We also had the captain of the All-American Trap Team. I think he had broken something like fourteen hundred and eighty straight clays."

Bob Sibley appeared at the door of the Doobissary, a heavy sandwich in his hand. "This is fresh lobster," he said. "You ought to have one."

It was a persuasive invitation to a man whose stomach had already contended with Holiday Inn and capsicum jerky. Sibley had flown the lobsters in from his home in Bradford, Massachusetts. A short, rotund man beneath a deerstalker's cap, Sibley had been in the life insurance business, but his passion was hunting grouse and woodcock over setters in the coverts of New Brunswick. Sibley had been shooting retriever trials for years. He relishes the companionship, fine shotguns, and, judging by the circumference of his belt, the refrigerator of the Doobissary.

So that their dogs could clearly see their marks, the handlers wanted long popper throws and fliers that carried, preferably above the horizon. The judges had called for flier falls at fifty yards. The guns were shooting at thirty-five, as momentum carried the bird another fifteen.

The guns got the credit for accurate shooting, but to a man they praised the throwers. At "Guns up!" the thrower reached into a large crate at his feet and removed the live bird. If it was a duck, a flight bird with strong wing muscles, the thrower grasped the two wings together close to the back and in a stepping motion smoothly pitched the duck into terminal flight. A pheasant, however, depends on its legs. Its wing muscles are weaker, designed for short bursts of flight. If held like a duck, a pheasant will cramp up and fly poorly, falling short. The throwers held the pheasants sideways, a leg and a wing gripped in one hand.

"To put those birds consistently in a tight circle," Dan Kingston said, "you have to have a good thrower to get that bird in a high arc. It's a combination of strength— a hard, hard throw—and consistency. You only get into problems when you have an erratic thrower."

There is Harvard in Kingston's vitae and a cultured manner in his lanky bearing. He tried running retrievers in trials, but gave it up—"Such a tough game"—and has been shooting in trials for forty years. Thinking of how the mechanics of field trial shooting lack the element of surprise, I asked him why it would be that difficult to hit a pheasant or duck thrown practically at one's side and flying away. "It seems to be the easiest shot, but it's tougher than it looks," he said, "particularly to drop those birds in a five- to ten-foot circle where the judges want them to fall. You start aiming, and thinking, and once you start thinking in wing shooting, you get into trouble. I don't know how much I lead the bird. I just shoot."

Sibley was once approached by a top shot from Maine for an invitation to gun at retriever trials. Bob threw him some pheasants. The man promptly missed two.

"It so alarmed him that we had to use a backup gun to settle him down," Sibley said. "Guys really get nervous at field trials. There's a lot of pressure not to miss—especially at the Nationals. These field trial people are out for *blood*.

God, the amount of money and time they invest in this game!"

The door of the Doobissary opened. Orlie Boehler stuck his head in and said, "Clive, we should be able to go to number fifty-seven before we switch guns. Is that okay with you?"

It was a warm afternoon. Clive was scrunched down on the couch, contemplating a nap. "I don't care," he said, "fine with me."

Trialers are, as they say, dog people, and clannish at that. The regulars all know each other and the work of the better retrievers. They share an affection for dogs and hunting and take pleasure in seeing and having a hand in "good dog work." They are forever discussing the complexities of training, problem dogs, problem tests, problem trialers. Gossip moves with the trucks, following the weekend trials north in the summer (Puget Sound Retriever Club Trial, Fort Collins, Westchester, Finger Lakes) and going south ahead of the ice (Chattanooga, Tar Heel, Blue Ridge, Palmetto) as dogs earn initials and trialers push the dogs, push themselves, down the road, into the night to a plywood motel where there's a glutinous mint on the boingboing pillow and someone has welded titanium wrap around the crappy little plastic highball glass in a closet john with a shower curtain that sticks to your butt instead of the wall and the waitress is not sure about "fahjeetahs" but can direct you to the barbershop where you can read *Guns & Ammo* if you're not distracted by the televised highlights of last week's high school football games while you count the keys on the guy's belt that is holding up the most humongous belly—God, for a drink! —then to assemble each June at the National Amateur and each November at the National Championship Stake.

English cavalry twill is rarely evident now in the galleries, but there is still a good deal of money behind many of the dogs. A Lab in this National was said to have fetched $40,000 in transferring his title. Some old money, much new money—but money nonetheless.

Pros charge upwards of three hundred fifty dollars a month to train retrievers. One pro is said to reach seven hundred fifty. Birds are always additional. Ducks are eight bucks a pop.

Patti Roberts will spend five to six months getting a young dog through the basics to the level of a dependable gun dog. To polish it into a competitive field trial retriever, Rick will then work on the dog month after month, and—his clients willing, as they seem to be—year after year. I once met a shellfish inspector, not exactly a man with Loden in his closet, who had put six thousand dollars in pro fees into his Golden. He didn't begrudge a dime of it. "It's not a cheap sport. I've been at this dog game for six years, and I've only got one blue ribbon. That's how hard it is. A really good dog comes around only once in a lifetime."

For a game with no money prizes—only ribbons, rosettes, pins, a trophy at the National—field trials draw a dedicated cadre, a good number of whom are fiercely competitive Type A's. When there are dogs on the line, egos are there too.

"I don't get much enjoyment out of driving five hundred miles and going out in the first series."

"This business of people being in field trials for the camaraderie is bullshit. I put twelve hundred miles a week down the road during trial season. I'm very competitive. I'd rather train dogs than field trial, but the trials are the end of it."

"People ought to be in this for the dogs, not the game. You should always be thinking of the dogs. They can get hurt."

"This desire to win can take over everything. It causes the dogs to suffer for it and suffer greatly. The dog doesn't know why he's getting bumped down."

"Is there a lot of money in field trials? Yes, and most of it is mine."

Rick Roberts said that field trials are exceedingly honest because there is no money involved. "You might get a judge who favors certain things, but that's as far as it goes. When I come home Sunday without winning anything, I never think it's because I was screwed. The dog or I did something wrong."

In the gallery, back of the rope, jokes that would have a remarkable shelf life throughout the trial (more than a few with lineage back to Chestertown) were getting a repetitive airing.

"What's the difference between a toy poodle and a pit bull humping your leg?"

"I've already heard it."

"You let the pit bull finish."

At trials people bring their canvas stools and aluminum chairs to the gallery, then drive off and forget them. A lapse of memory at the Shoreline trial in Connecticut is repaired the next week at the Maine Retriever Trial at

Skowhegan. At any time in the trial season there is a considerable inventory of furniture in the trucks and station wagons of involuntary bailees on the way back to reunion. Gallery seatings are shifting arrangements of generous license, possession still being nine tenths of the law. You leave for the Porta Potties, return dispossessed, find an empty chair, and sit down. The owner appears. "That's okay, stay where you are. I'll let you know."

Bill and Ginny Atterbury stood at the rear of the gallery and watched Jay Sweezey walk B. B. Powder to the line. Bill was a lawyer and is now retired, a polite, warm man with a mustache on his lip. His father owned the Pennsylvania Railroad. Bill and Ginny's first dogs were English pointers, over which they hunted pheasants and chukar partridge in Idaho. "We also hunt quail in Florida," Ginny said, "but southern Florida has too many rattle-snakes. And water mocassins. We've been running Labs in field trials for about ten years. I doubt that we'll stay for the end of this National. Of course, if we had some close friends here, that would be another story."

B. B. sat at the line watching the birds go. Dennis Bath said, "Number fifty-six," and Sweezey leaned over, bending his left knee in to draw her shoulders toward him, lining her backbone for the flier. B. B. needed no help. She ran straight to the pheasant and returned with it, and when sent for the memory bird she drove between the guns and the pheasant, made a sudden cut to the right and picked it up.

As B. B. trotted back through the gully, mouth full of pheasant, Sweezey glanced over his left shoulder at the position of the sun. If he had to handle B. B. on the blind retrieve, she would be looking into the sun. He did not have to whistle. B. B. ran straight out three hundred yards to the bird.

The gallery applauded. Sweezey stopped briefly to chat with the Atterburys and walked back to his truck to put B. B. away.

"You never know," he said. "This is the twenty-fifth National I've run. Never won one. It's tough. Just goddamned luck. But it's nice starting off strong. Smokey screwed it up. B. B. was lucky on that flier—it fell short, and she came up on it. And with the memory bird, she came out of the pond and hooked around. The guns held her, and there it was. Well, I gotta take care of my dogs."

He drove off down the fence line, parked in a field, and began letting his dogs out to air them.

*T*o THE skeptical reader desiring credentials, here's my badge: I have competed in a field trial. Actually, it was one test. And the trial was informal. Okay, so it wasn't much of a retrieve, either. My dog and I provided entertainment for the gallery, but I can't say that our foray to the line attracted further invitations.

It happened this way. Some years ago, wanting to learn how to get my first Lab—a pup named Ben, no initials— beyond obedience and into reliable retrieving, I sought out advice. This led me to a small sign at the edge of a road on the Eastern Shore. The sign read: FIELD TRIAL. I turned off the highway and followed a succession of arrows through the woods and out to a fan of trucks and station wagons parked at the edge of an immense stubble field of corn. People were walking about with whistles hanging from their necks and dogs at their sides. I got Ben out of his crate, snapped on his lead, and attempted an impression of a retriever person.

If pride goeth before a fall, mine certainly wenteth. The bait was placed by the sort of casual inquiry that field trialers use to smoke out the weekend klutz.

"Does your dog retrieve?"

The jig was up. As a retriever person, I was hardly to the larval stage. Did Ben retrieve? From the woodpile he distributed splits of oak around the yard. He retrieved our socks, our shoes, our house guests' embarrassments. Until Ben, my experience with dogs had been limited to an Irish setter so delinquently bonkers that my grandfather had forbidden his presence on hunts, and a dachshund who defied mortality and peed on the rug. Ben would be different. Ben would be obedient, he would hunt. Ben would do calculus.

"Does my dog retrieve? Sure."

The derby stake was for young dogs, so I entered him. My wife was of the opinion that I had taken leave of reality. Having no idea what I was supposed to do, I watched the other dogs retrieve. The test was a single mark, if you can describe as a mark a dead pigeon thrown by a tiny figure who appeared to be at least a mile away. It was evident that I was in a serious poolroom with deadly shooters. The other dogs may as well have had names like Vinny and Killer. They leaned against lamp posts and spit in the gutter. They were lean, aggressive rockets, about as soft as gneiss. If these were pups, I was Mahatma Ghandi.

When Ben's name was announced, I walked him to the line and said sit. Slowly Ben sat. He looked up at me in all his puppy softness. This was ridiculous. In a sympathetic voice that implied it would be no disgrace to back out now, the judge asked if I was ready, and for reasons inexplicable to the sensible mind what came out of my mouth was, "Yes!" At that distance the gun made a sound like "pap," and an object the size of a pea fell somewhere in the largest field in North America.

I said, "Fetch!"

Ben trotted out about fifteen feet and began making circling moves indicating that he was about to do some marking of a different sort. The judge yelled to the guns, "Help him out!" The guns yelled, "Hey, hey, hey!" Ben galloped out maybe fifty feet, went into his disengaged mode, squatted; the guns yelled heyheyheyheyhey, he ran some more, reconsidered, stopped to examine a corncob, peed on a dirt clod. He eventually reached the rough proximity of the guns, where he piddled around for what seemed like the better part of the afternoon until he stumbled upon the dead pigeon. He did some investigative sniffing. He picked up the bird by the tip of its wing as though it were a claymore mine.

I began yelling victoriously, right through the rule book. "Ben! Ben, come! Come! Come ON! COME ON, FELLA! COME ON, BEN, THAT'S THE STUFF, BOY, *COME ON!* Dog trainers advise commands of brevity. I was working my way into an essay. But I'll be go-to-hell, he had the damned pigeon and he was bringing it right to me! I considered the possibilities of a press conference, where I would accept the trophy, the accolades, while, of course, appearing modest before the cameras as I gave advice to the handlers huddled at my feet.

Ben galloped by me in triumph, past the judges and the gallery, and into the woods, where he proceeded to eat the pigeon.

I went home and bought James Lamb Free's *Training Your Retriever*, the same book that got Dottie Metcalf started—with different results. I also bought a retrieving bumper, which looked like a salami of squeezable plastic, and tied on a short throwing rope. Free described the "Baseball Diamond Method of Teaching Hand Signals." He said to imagine a baseball diamond. I took his advice literally. I walked Ben to a nearby school and sat him on the pitcher's mound. Following Free's instructions, I threw the bumper toward second, left Ben on the mound, returned to home plate. I raised my arm and yelled, "Back!" In time, I extended these casts to the right (first base) and left (third base).

If trained often enough, Free wrote, you can eventually hide the bumpers and the dog will go on the command alone. Which Ben did—when it suited him, or when there was compelling evidence (the honking above the blind, the gunfire) that there was warm goose out on the river.

Despite my limited talents, Ben was an eager hunter and dependable retriever. But his enthusiasm for blind retrieves could be measured by stones. And he considered steadiness to be an academic exercise. When the grouse and the guns went off in the opaque thickets of West Virginia, Ben took off as well, in whatever direction inspired him. "Steady to Wing and Shot" was not on his license plate.

In searching for another pup during Ben's declining years, I was drawn to a number of weekend field trials and eventually the National in Oklahoma. If I saw retrievers at the line bounce like yo-yos, there were also retrievers steady as oaks that marked and remembered the falls of numerous birds at distances requiring magnification by Zeiss, that went from a dead run to statuary at the sound of the whistle, that took any variety of casts to God knows where and retrieved with a firm but gentle mouth. I saw dogs do all that with style and eagerness, then sit stoically by and honor another dog as the birds went up and the honored dog went out.

This wasn't my game, but I envied the moves, and I wanted to learn more about how one trains a retriever to do what those dogs did.

In 1948, Jay Sweezey bought his first retriever. He had finished a hitch in the Coast Guard and two years at Columbia University and had been "busting his hump" fishing for mackerel, tuna, swordfish, and cod. He wanted a Chesapeake. Another fisherman, named Hutch, told him that he ought to get a Lab, that he could have his if he'd pay the accumulated vet bills. For fifty dollars Jay cleared Hutch's account and bought the Lab. He started "playing with her," teaching her the rudiments of ducking work. Sweezey then drove a '41 Plymouth coupe. The seat fell forward, and in the compartment behind it he put the dog. From the newspaper he learned about an upcoming field trial near where he lived on Long Island. He drove over to watch. "This looks easy," he concluded. "Hell, I can do that."

He took his dog home and began emulating what he had seen in the trial, using sticks as retrieving bumpers. He discovered that getting retrievers to do his bidding was more difficult than he had imagined.

Sweezey ran his first field trial in 1952. He bred the bitch, kept one of the pups, trained him, and entered trials. The dog earned its initials. Sweezey ran him in the 1956 National at Weldon Spring, Missouri. FC El Jay Ace Scenter.

Some weeks before the National, I found the Sweezeys' Cape Cod house in the Eastern Shore woods outside of Chestertown. At seven in the morning in early fall, as Kay Sweezey was leaving to teach first grade, Jay's pickup and trailer flew down the drive, gravel whanging against the wheel wells. Aluminum crates full of ducks and cooing pigeons were lashed to the roof of his truck box with rubber bungee straps. Highway departments want pigeons out from under their underpasses. Farmers with guano-covered hay bales in the loft want "barnies" gone from their barns. Like Rick and Patti Roberts, Sweezey holds his pigeon sources close to his chest. Pigeons cost up to two dollars a bird. Sweezey spends twelve hundred dollars a year on duck and pigeon feed.

As Sweezey sped down the road, hundreds of Canada geese rose off the Chester River, breaking into echelons, gabbling, filing their flight plans to the corn and soybean fields.

Sweezey trains on different farms, moving his dogs from field to field, pond to pond. He pulled into a harvested cornfield and went to work. In a low drainage, he dropped a sack of dead pigeons for the blind retrieves, then drove up the slope some distance away and parked.

He began opening kennel doors to let the dogs out to air, the bitches separately from the males. He doesn't abide fights. He is especially watchful of the big alpha males, the macho boys that cock their legs over their backs as though they could write their initials on his cab window. More than a dozen black Labs leapt from confinement and bounded around the field.

Sweezey reads dogs, talks dogs. "I love them up, but separately. Never when the pack is out. Surest way to start a fight. A moody bitch is a pain in the ass. I should know, I've had a number of them. If you see a dog in the neighborhood, with its tail down, slinking, looking left and right, that's a stranger. You see a dog walking upright, pissing on all the porches, that dog lives in the neighborhood.

"A good trainer can get extra effort out of mediocre dogs, but a top dog can make any trainer look awfully good. People send a dog to a trainer and think they're going to have a dog that can type and use the phone."

The Labs chased each other around the cornfield, racing, colliding, tumbling, wrestling, a grand canine recess of pink tongues and white teeth against an animated field of black.

Sweezey placed an aluminum pan on the ground below the trailer spigot and filled it with water. "Three-quart pudding pans. I buy them from hotel supply stores. Much cheaper than stainless." The spigot protruded from the bottom of the trailer forward of the tires—forty gallons of water between the axles. Traveling the trial circuit like a pilot with a map of emergency strips circled in red and strapped to the thigh, Sweezey is constantly vigilant for sources of water for his dogs. He prefers well water when he can get it, worries about treated town water, softened water. "It loosens up my dogs." He smells it first, has a taste, then takes what he can get, at gas stations mostly. At night the station owners often remove the spigot handle. Sweezey carries a plumber's Sillcocks key, fits it over the valve stem, and gets his water. At the National in Oklahoma, he tanked up at a nursery in Duncan. "You can never get enough water."

Sweezey laid a braided cotton rug over the hood. Like a surgeon after scrubbing, he then arranged some of the instruments of his trade: two starter pistols, a box of blank .22 cartridges, a leather bag of twenty-gauge shotgun shells, a double-barreled Rizzini, a Tri-Tronics electronic collar and transmitter, an electric cattle prod, and a coiled, braided whip.

He switched on the radio in the cab and rolled down the windows. "Spanish Eyes" floated out. "You don't hear those good old songs any more."

Sweezey called the dogs back to their holes in the box. Some of the kennels were nearly five feet off the ground. To help those dogs get a grip leaping up, he wedged in the openings a heavy dowel from which hung a panel of Astro-Turf.

"Chub! Here! Here, Chub! CHUB!! Slick, okay, baby, good girl. Slick? *Slick!* Buck. Buckley! Kennel, Buckley. Alll *Riiiight!* Hi, Sweets. Come on Weevils. What do you think, girl? Good girl. Sure you're a good girl, come on now. *Good girl!*

A big male jumped into his kennel. "Goddamn, I like that dog's rear end. Like Smithfield hams." Sweezey looks for a "good bottom" in the dogs he buys for his clients. "That's a horse term. It means good legs, underpinnings, and a good engine in the rear. I like a dog to *drive*, especially on blinds. I don't care if they're ten or twelve feet off the line, just so long as they're driving. I want to keep their confidence up. Dennis Bath and Tony Snow like long marks and tough angles. You've got to get your dogs stretched out. You need a dog with lots of momentum that can carry for those long falls."

The Labs came in reluctantly, panting. Sweezey checked an ear, lifted a tail, inspecting for worms, pivoting this way and that as dog after dog went to den.

"I like to see a dog look healthy," he said. "You have to keep them free of parasites."

At the 1959 National in Reno, the alkali water gave the dogs diarrhea. "It was coming out of them like Flit out of a gun. Cotton Pershall told me about kneading wheat bread in with cooked chopped meat. It hardened them right up. Cottage cheese is also good. It has a good bacteria."

At trials, Sweezey can be found each evening at the rear deck of his trailer preparing supper for his dogs. He mixes a little canned food for flavor in with the kibbel. After the dogs have eaten, he pours soapy water into a large bin and washes the dinner bowls.

Bill Snyder, a neighbor, was helping Sweezey with his training. After Snyder shot flier pigeons all morning for the dogs, Sweezey drove to another farm and sent Snyder out to a brush pile in a cornfield with a crate of mallards. A flier, he said, gets a dog up for his work. Sweezey handed me a starter pistol, a netted bag of dead pigeons, and a stool and directed me out across the cornfield, stopping me short of Snyder.

Sweezey got a dog from the truck and strapped the electronic collar around his neck. At the base of the collar was a black radio receiver the size of a bar of soap, into which was screwed a short rubber-flex antenna. Two contact points underneath the receiver pressed against the dog's neck. The transmitter looked like a flashlight. Sweezey stuck it into his hip pocket.

Snyder had lost his concentration. He threw up the first mallard, and shot, and it flew away.

Sweezey said, "Goddamn!"

Snyder missed the second one and the third, which flew far out into the field and landed. Sweezey sent the dog. The dog ran well beyond the duck. Sweezey pulled a collapsible antenna up from the transmitter, blew his whistle, yelled "*No!*" and punched a button on the transmitter. The Lab yelped. Sweezey walked toward the dog and handled him with whistle blasts and casts toward the duck. The duck flew away. When the dog came in, Sweezey got down on one knee. "Okay, boy, that's okay," he said soothingly, patting the dog.

He let out another dog that promptly jumped up on the truck to get at the birds in their crates. "Outlaw son of a bitch! He can always screw things up."

Snyder missed the fourth duck. Thirty-two dollars, not counting feed, had just flown to the Chesapeake Bay. "Okay, Bill, that's it!" Jay yelled. "Come on in." He handed Snyder a sack of dead pigeons and sent him back out to pop.

I was no improvement. Throwing poppers looked rather simple. When Sweezey threw a dead bird—even a heavy duck or pheasant—he stepped effortlessly, his backswing a smooth figure eight, and sent the bird into migration. I gripped the wings as he had demonstrated and at his signal fired the pistol, stepped from the rubber, and pitched: a tight-grip knuckle ball. The pigeon rose straight into the air and fell a few feet away. No bird. On my slider, the slick wing feathers slipped through my fingers, and the pigeon skimmed the corn stubble low on the deck. I was grateful not to have a collar around my neck.

Before sending each dog for our poppers, Sweezey would pull a live duck from under his arm and put it into flight. Up came the Rizzini. After the dog retrieved its marks, Sweezey would turn and send him off in a lateral direction deep to a blind pile of blaze-orange bumpers. (Dogs are color blind.) When Sweezey shouted "Back!", a sharp echo detonated from the woods. The leaves were turning. Russet maples, yellow tulip poplars. The pines were dark. There were geese overhead, their wings cupped, webbed feet out, on final to the corn.

After lunch at a cafe in town, Sweezey drove to another farm and parked by a pond. He removed a pair of blue rain pants from the breezeway and put them on. He opened a kennel door—"Here Snoop"—and threw a bumper into the pond. Snoopy leaped in after it.

When the dog returned, Sweezey squirted a green bead of Palmolive dishwashing detergent down Snoopy's wet back and lathered him up. Sweezey threw the bumper back into the pond. Snoop splashed in and retrieved it. Sweezey squeegeed off the suds with his broad hands and threw the bumper back into the water. In went Snoop. Sweezey squeegeed off more suds, threw the bumper, squeegeed, threw, until Snoop had taken enough circuits through the rinse cycle that his coat squeaked. Snoopy would be returning to his owner that night by an airplane out of Baltimore.

As Sweezey worked over the dog, he talked with him. "Good boy, huh, son? That's it, good guy, come on son." Snoopy shook. Jay put him away. "People rub their dogs down with towels, and all they're doing is working that water into the undercoat. Labs will shake most of it off."

The trainer who most influenced Sweezey was Charles Morgan of Random Lake, Wisconsin. Morgan was a modest man and an experienced trainer. He won the 1950 National with one of the four Goldens ever to win a National. "Chuck Morgan got more out of ordinary and problem dogs than any man I know. His kennel was an old fox farm with a hundred runs. He was always about three days from a Gillette. He wore white painter coveralls, and there were always paw prints on his chest from the dogs leaping on him. After dinner he'd wipe bacon grease from his big Sunbeam skillet with a piece of bread and go out to the kennel. He'd turn on the floodlights and walk around talking with the dogs. If there was one he'd been hard on that day, he'd give him a piece of that greasy bread and softly sweet-talk him.

"Most of these people at trials you rarely see pat a dog. But I believe in giving them a little pat. You have to have hands on the dog. But I don't put up with any bullshit, either. I don't believe in nitpicking them all the time. When I get on them, I get on them *hard*. I'll take off a little hide with that whip."

The training methods of the field trialers I observed were wide variations of teaching, repetition, encouragement, and punishment. They all were of the emphatic belief that a good trainer must have a sixth sense in being able to read dogs, understand their personalities and moods, know when to lean (and how hard) and when to lay off. I saw dogs petted—and I saw one hesitant about going into the water on a blind retrieve yanked off the ground by its choke collar and jabbed in the groin with an electric cattle prod.

"Retriever training is an empirical thing," Sweezey said. "Dogs are creatures of habit. A lot of these amateur folks come up with basic obedience problems. It's because there's too much softball. If you want to play this game and win, you'd better be prepared to play hardball."

Retriever field trialers speak often of pressure. They are not referring to their own fear of goofing in front of their peers. They mean the pressure the dogs are under during training. Pressure is a euphemism—for punishment, the threat of punishment, the fear of punishment. Trainers refer to punishment as "correction," which in dog training, as in child rearing, is accurate enough in its context.

But correction does not exactly describe the instruments of punishment among trainers of the old school for serious infractions. When the dog was close they used the boot, the whip, a length of chain, the butt of a shotgun, the prod. When the dog was well beyond reach, trainers ran out into the field and shook the dog, pounded him, used whatever they had thought to bring with them.

The disadvantage was that dogs have short memories. Often by the time the trainer got out there, the dog had forgotten what he was being punished for. Once a dog was way out in what Sweezey calls the "fuck you" area and was "giving you the pickle," a trainer of the old school would raise his shotgun and let fly a charge of birdshot. This was referred to as stinging the dog. Sprinkling the dog. Touching the dog.

Stinging a dog with light shot was hardly a publicized technique—although it is mentioned in some books by pros—because it required great skill, judgment, and experience with shotguns to avoid breaking the skin and seriously injuring the animal. Shotgun "correction" was now in the closet, and in there with it were a great many trainers of the distance runners, the pointing breeds.

The experienced pros used light loads in smaller gauge, open-bored guns. (For closer range correction, they carried rat shot—a pinch of extremely fine shot pellets—in a smooth-bored .22 pistol.) When a dog consistently gave them the pickle, they walked off sixty yards, planted a marker in the field, and sent the dog again. When the dog passed the flag and disobeyed the command, the trainer shot.

Once was usually enough. After that, just the sound of a charge of birdshot over the dog's head was sufficient correction.

But things could go wrong. Trainers could err in judgment, miscalculate the range, misjudge the speed of the dog, inadvertently mix duck loads with their training shells and drop a high-brass #4 in the chamber instead of light #9s, or fire the full choke barrel rather than the open bore. Trainers could lose their tempers. And dogs could turn their heads just as the shot pattern arrived. Trainers tell of having seen retrievers at trials with one white eye, of being embarrassed to bring their dog into the vet for hip X-rays and having to explain all the white dots on the radiograph. Some dogs had to be buried.

At the Swampdog trial in Pennsylvania, Sweezey said, "A shotgun can be very effective without seriously harming the dog, but I don't use one any longer. I'll bet I am the only pro at this trial with a slingshot in his pocket. In training I'll use it to show a dog where the bird is in the water. If he's really hard-headed I'll send a marble by him. They really hear it buzz by. And sometimes I'll hit them, but I don't want to hurt a dog."

Sweezey was walking a Lab back from a test when the dog, sensing that Sweezey was sufficently distracted, ran off to anoint tires in the parking lot. Sweezey yelled his name, futilely. "Goddamn him!" He pulled a small aluminum slingshot from his coat pocket, the marbles clicking. The dog undoubtedly heard them. He reappeared from around a truck bumper, ears down, contrite. Sweezey put the slingshot back into his pocket.

Rick and Patti Roberts live an hour or so south of Sweezey. The front of their property is cratered with pits once borrowed by the highway department for the paving of Route 50. The water table is conveniently at the surface. It fills the borrow pits, making retriever ponds. Patti often works the young dogs there.

She threw a "happy bumper" into the water for Cappy. "I start with happy bumpers to get them up." Cappy was hesitant, dropped the happy bumper, wasn't happy. "Here, Cap, hold." Patti put it into his mouth and patted him under the chin, brought him again to heel, and removed the bumper. She had set up a short "single T"; a pile of bumpers twenty yards out and two piles of bumpers on either side, nearer in. They were in weeds. Blind retrieves.

"Back!"

Cappy went out a few yards and "popped"—sat down and looked back at her, head down. She pressed the button on the collar transmitter, "nicked" him. Cappy yipped. "Back! *Back!*" He ran to the pile and retrieved a bumper.

"I have to force him at first," Patti said. "A lot of these dogs are hard to get started. This is a lot of pressure. They have to do it because they're told, and a lot of dogs can't handle that. Eventually they'll do it because they like it. Now Bo is real dumb and happy, whereas Cappy is cautious and cerebral. Some young dogs sitting at heel keep looking down, or up, or left or right. We call that bugging. In their little pea-brains, they think if they don't look where you want them to—straight ahead—then they don't have to go. It just shows how much they don't want to do blinds."

After a few more retrieves and some handles, Cappy was going with enthusiasm.

"Good *dooogggggg!* Good dog, Cappy, good boy!"

Patti works her young dogs on fifteen-, twenty-, and thirty-foot check cords of braided polypropylene. She gets rope burns across the backs of her legs from cords whipping behind unchecked Labs. On occasion she has been flipped into the air. She works stooped over a great deal, the pups between her knees—"Hold, Cappy, hold!"—and submerges her back spasms at night in the whirlpool.

Patti Roberts is direct, her eyes hazel, her short hair the color of sandstone. Green Wellingtons came to her knees over Levis. There was strength in her arms. On her hands were black fingerless gloves (Rick wears white deerskin bronc gloves he buys in volume from a rodeo supplier in New York). She was wearing a tee shirt advertising Green Mountain, Vermont. During the heat of August, she and Rick take their string of dogs north to train near Stowe. Among the prints of waterfowl and dogs on the log walls of their house is a small framed medallion that is inscribed *1983 National Retriever Championship Stake, Patricia Roberts, Judge*. She and Rick turned pro the day after that National concluded.

Patti grew up in Williamsville, New York, a suburb of Buffalo. Her father, a lawyer and avid hunter, told the boys at the duck club that he was bringing his little girl to hunt. They said not in our club. He told them what they could do with their decoys, quit the club, and found his own places to hunt with her. When Patti was twelve, he gave her a black Lab bitch and on weekends took her and the dog to a trainer in Niagara Falls. Training was progressing well until the dog was introduced to her first shackled duck, a live mallard trussed in a harness. The dog balked.

"That did it," Patti said. "I bought two ducks and started training her at home to retrieve them."

Patti was out on the marsh one day helping her father brush the duck blind when she heard some shooting nearby. The waterfowl season hadn't yet opened. She followed her curiosity over to a scene of white coats and black dogs. The dog work impressed on her young mind the possibilities of canine intelligence and accelerated her interest in what she was discovering she loved most—training retrievers.

Soon enough she met a big man with Maryland plates on his truck who was training retrievers for the trials in western New York. Patti asked if she could be his bird boy, and Jay Sweezey said sure. She was thirteen. A year later Patti entered her first field trial. Her Lab didn't make the call-backs.

Each September Patti bagged birds for Sweezey, placing blinds, firing poppers, and helping take care of the dogs. She worked for a local veterinarian, and when she entered SUNY at Delhi she studied to be a vet technician, majoring in small animal science and minoring in large animal camouflage, hiding her Lab with the dorm supervisor. She returned from college to work for the vet and live in the country with two Labs.

"You can't train dogs in Buffalo in winter, so I put a couple of dogs with Jay. I heard that you could make good money hot-walking race horses in South Carolina, so I went down there, but I couldn't get the job and ran out of money. When the snakes came out I left for Maryland."

As director of the Talbot County Humane Society, Patti started attending obedience trials and bench shows. She thought the dogs looked as bored as she was. She would wander around in the parking lots, looking into cars to see if there were animals in stress. She broke some car windows rescuing dogs from heat prostration. She says that her experience with the politics of the Humane Society "helped mature me in the temper department."

Mindful of the ironies of mercy, Patti was not impressed that Canadian field trials no longer allowed the shooting of live birds. Canadian poppers on occasion have gotten so green by the end of the trial that bird stewards have stuffed them with ping pong balls to get them to float. They have been known to achieve popper status by having their heads placed in a contraption that presses a nail into the bird's brain. "That's humane and shooting isn't?"

Bo took off before Patti gave a command. She blew her whistle. He sat and yelped as she punched the button. Bo looked down to his left.

"Come on, Bo, look at me . . . *Look at me!* Over!"

Bo didn't go over, he swung his head looking left and right. Patti walked toward him.

"Look at me. *Look* at me. *Bo, look at me!*" Patti nicked him again. He looked at her. "Over!" Bo went over, got the bumper, and returned to her side.

Buster was yipping as he walked at heel. There was no collar around his neck, only the memory of it and a long check cord that Patti held as she made turns, reverses, and halts.

"Instead of doing the right thing and obeying commands, Buster panics. You don't ever want to burn them and not get the right response. You're just a big wimp, aren't you, Buster?" He soon quieted down. "Good boy, okay, Buster. This type of dog is the easiest dog to ruin if you don't know what you're doing and lean on him. If he's not overpressured, he will grow out of it."

Once a retriever's permanent teeth grow in (around seven months) and he has discovered the fun of elementary retrieving and understands simple commands taught largely through encouragement and play—here, heel, sit—boot camp begins. Trainers call it force fetching, or force training.

By briefly pinching the ear, they force the dog to open its mouth and hold the bumper for as long as the trainer demands. "One of the most difficult things for pups to learn is to *hold* that bumper," Patti said. "It's their first negative command."

The next step is getting the dog, again by ear pinch, to take the bumper from the hand, and finally—a big step—off the ground.

Patti then works the dogs at picking up odd objects: a pop bottle wrapped with gaffer tape, a large metal spoon, then a dead pigeon. As she graduates from ear pinch to slingshot to switch, the dog is going for a thrown bumper and finally for nothing evident—on blinds. Force fetching of retrievers seemed to me less cruel than oxymoronic. Why force a retriever to do what it naturally wants to do anyway?

The answer defines the relationship between handler and dog: handlers want retrievers to obey their bidding at all times. They emphasize that this is essential not only to the field trialer but also to the hunter, who can lose downed birds when his dog—not having seen the fall—refuses to enter the river or drive deep into thick cover.

"These young dogs easily get into the habit of being sloppy," Patti said. "I want them to get into the habit of being good. You've got to know when to apply pressure and more importantly, when to stop. A lot of sloppy, wimpy retrievers come out of that with force fetch. They learn what retrieving is all about. And then they start loving it."

There are some things retrievers don't want to do. They will throw a kink in a straight line retrieve to avoid having to cross a ditch or road, or enter water or cover, on the oblique. They prefer to "square" obstacles, or they just go down the road, down the ditch. Some dogs refuse to pick up woodcock, others won't touch soggy birds. Dottie Metcalf's Megan had flown so fast through force fetch that Patti had skipped the odd objects (the bottle, spoon, and bird). Then one day Megan bounded up to a retrieving bumper covered with sand. Whoa, not in my mouth. Wouldn't pick it up. Patti had to start Megan all over with force fetch.

Patti was training a young Chesapeake that retrieved with spirit, but on Chessie terms, holding the bumper so tightly she wouldn't give it up. The bumper would some day be a bird. Crunch. With this bitch Patti would have to work long on "Drop!"

Steadiness does not come naturally to hunting dogs. Pointers and setters are known for disappearing over the horizon searching for scent, the hunter usually far behind, hunting for the dog. It can take persistent training to get them steady ("staunched"), particularly when honoring ("backing") the first dog that makes point. And despite retrievers' reputations as water dogs, many of them aren't crazy about leaping into an icy lake in winter without the stimulation of a duck shot before them. When they swim past an island or a point, they want to "dock," get out on land. Cold water blinds are the destination of all force training of retrievers, the toughest test of a handler's control of the dog.

The modern route is by way of the electronic collar.

For many young retrievers, force training culminates in their "introduction to the collar." Patti and Rick Roberts make no such introductions until the dog is first properly trained. As with any effective dog training, collar work has to be done gradually, step by step, over and over. By plugging different resistors into the receiver, the trainer can deliver a message to the dog that varies from a tingle to a jolt.

Tri-Tronics, the company in Tucson, Arizona, that makes the most popular electronic collars, does not use the words "shock" or "pain" in its literature, preferring instead to speak of their "remote trainer" as providing "electrical stimulation." The newer models emit a short buzzing sound before the dog gets stimulated, followed by a tone when the current stops. For minor corrections, the trainer can press a button that emits only the buzz. Sometimes that is stimulation enough. Another button emits only the "good dog" tone. The concept is to go beyond strictly punishment training—the electronic two-by-four—and get the dog to avoid problems and feel relieved and happy when he has.

The electronic collar transformed dog training. In field trials it finally gave the amateurs a run against the pros. It allowed trainers, women especially, who could not handle big dogs, or could not bear to do to dogs what the physical trainers did, to get into the game. And it changed the game, brought so many more highly trained dogs to the line that judges had to devise increasingly difficult, artificial tests just to reduce the field so that a weekend trial could be concluded in three days. It helped drive field trials further from hunting.

If electronic collars gave handlers the distinct advantage of instant correction when their dogs were well beyond shotgun range, the disadvantage was that they were too easy to use. The collar was soon in the hands of people who wanted shortcuts to blue ribbons, who didn't understand dogs or training, who saw themselves as having a device in their hands that would transform Duke the Dork into Duke the Wonder Dog.

Dog giving you the pickle? Zap.

Many dogs were psychologically ruined by the collar, and still are, by people who do not learn how to use it properly, who have short fuses, who have never come to appreciate that dog training requires years of experience in understanding how dogs think. Some dogs go wild when tickled. Others are "clammers"—they tighten up, get sullen, and appear not to respond to electricity. Handlers can mistake clammers for being tough dogs. They put the heat on and ruin what are in fact hypersensitive retrievers.

Particularly during the 1960s, when the collar became widespread in training, terms of derision ricocheted across the grounds at retriever field trials. Collar dogs. Electric dogs. Plodders. Pigs. Camels. Goats.

But piggy retrievers didn't overrun falls and refuse casts. They were careful, methodical, mechanical—unbelievably boring and unstylish in the eyes of the old schoolers like Jay Sweezey, who calls them "sleepwalkers." But sleepwalkers got the birds and they won trials. For a time, judges were prejudiced against collar-trained dogs, irritated that all the style and enthusiasm of retrieving was being lost. With his disdain for collar dogs, Sweezey uses the collar simply as punishment—to push a dog off a point, or back into the water—certainly not, in the idiom of the new school curricula, as a "total collar program." It is just one more tool on the hood of his truck.

The collar school and the old school are mostly friends, but of a small campus, and their opinions on this subject whir across the commons like the shrapnel of academe.

"Those electric dogs are too automated," Sweezey says, "kept to this distinct line. I want a dog to get out there and roll, even though he's not on a true azimuth. You're dealing with an animate being, and when you start blowing, casting, blowing, casting, before you know it they're turning around and checking in with you—popping. That little bitch I just got runs like a typical electric dog. Her tail is at twenty after four. She always seems like she's under restraint. The rule book says style, but half those electric dogs don't have that. They don't run out there full tilt. Some of them are pretty well scorched down. The whole game is different now. Everything is control. I want to see something with class and style."

"Their tails aren't up and cracking. The animation isn't there."

"He gets real oinky when you put the heat on."

"She gets goaty."

"He looks owly."

"The guy who invented the electronic collar should have been hung from the highest tree. That collar dog is scared to make a mistake. I never had a dog that didn't go out hard and fast."

"He can say all he wants against electric dogs, but I have seen some real piggy dogs come off his truck."

"Some of the people who complain of the collar don't think of what the physical trainers do to dogs. I've heard of dogs knocked cold. I have seen dogs strung up, rope over a tree limb, their rear toes just off the ground, and prodded. No one wants to see that."

"I've seen guys drag dogs into the water behind a motorcycle when they wouldn't go in on 'Back.' Nobody wants that."

"The collar is an easier way to ruin a dog than any other way of training," says Judy Aycock, one of the most proficient of collar trainers. "If you don't know how to use it, you ingrain too many wrong concepts into the dog. Some of these guys blame trouble on the collar rather than on their ignorance of how to use it properly. They'll throw a bird, and when the dog goes off the wrong way, they burn him. They think the dog knows what he should be doing, is disobeying and has to be corrected. Well, there are dozens of reasons why the dog hunted behind the guns. The wind may have pushed him; maybe he followed a ditch or didn't see the mark. Often the dog makes mistakes for a good reason, not because he's just contrary and is defying you. Why does he run the bank? He wants to, it's his nature. The dog has to be taught what is expected of him before you can start using the collar as reinforcement. Otherwise the dog will reach the wrong conclusion."

When Sweezey speaks of "that school of total electric control," he is referring to one headmaster and his students: Rex Carr of Escalon, California. Carr has never competed in a field trial and never will, but he is without equal for raising retrievers and handlers to the top of the game.

"When the electronic collar first came out, it took some style and desire out of the dogs," Tony Snow said. "I don't think that's true today. The control we have with collars on blinds now is so much more than it was under the old ways. I really don't like an unstylish dog. I saw that Rex Carr's dogs were stylish and yet were collar trained."

Rex Carr is seventy-seven. He rises at four in the morning and doesn't quit training until the sun is well below the ironed horizon of the San Joaquin Valley. At 10:00 P.M. he stops entering the day's dog performances in his computer, removes the telephone from its cradle, and goes to bed.

Escalon, where he lives (Carr-Lab Kennels), is an extended intersection between Stockton and Modesto near the eastern edge of the valley, where the foothills of the Sierra Nevada come up off the floor. By the toe of those slopes on any day but Saturday and Sunday, Rex's martial commands can be heard cutting through the winter fog and hot summer air, handling the dogs, handling the handlers.

"No! Julie, *No!* After you blow that whistle you *wait!* One thousand and one. One thousand and two. One thousand and three. Allow the dog to shift into neutral before shifting into high. *Then* give him 'Back.' Now he's got new momentum."

Rex sat in a plastic-webbed chair in a dry stubble field, a clipboard in his lap. He gave the appearance of a trail boss, indelibly weathered. The temperature was ninety-five degrees, San Joaquin caloric. A floppy tennis hat shaded his tan face. Beneath the hat was wiry white hair. The rare times he removed his steel-rimmed dark glasses, he revealed blue eyes. His shirt was white, western style with pearl snap buttons, and he was wearing construction boots.

Parked nearby in the shade of a solitary willow was Rex's truck—a big cab-over-engine Ford ton and a half. An exterior air conditioner the size of a suitcase was bolted to the roof. After a quarter century, the Ford had demonstrably rusted through its green paint. It looked like a Coke truck that had been parked too long in the Bronx. Its sides were a hive of twenty-six bins, into which Rex slides stainless steel kennels with small, fixed slits in the doors that admit only air. The darkness has a purpose: Rex wants his dogs quiet and relaxed in there.

Inside the dogs were quiet. They came off that truck with alacrity.

Nearby were ponds that Rex had designed to put dogs up against formidable obstacles: channels, points, dog-legs, islands, T-shaped peninsulas, all constructed of hard-pan scraped up near his cow sheds. Although he complained of judges "who don't know how to test in here at 150 yards, so they add distance to complicate it," the degree of complication now seen in field trial tests indirectly has some connection to Rex's own ambitions. As one former client said, Rex likes dogs that push the frontiers of the sport, "that do what you don't expect of even good dogs." There are Carr ponds at Dottie Metcalf's and Augie Belmont's farms, the Roberts's, the Aycocks' place. And his techniques are everywhere in the game.

Rex first got "all cranked up about retrievers" when he read an article in *Life* on the subject by Paul Bakewell while recovering from leg wounds he received from artillery shrapnel during the battle for Okinawa. Once out of Letterman General (he was in hospitals nearly a year), Rex moved to Escalon and bought a Lab. He tried raising grapes but gave it up.

"I don't think I saw my first field trial until 1948, but I boned up on them real fast," Rex said. "I knew my strengths. I didn't want to be a country doctor, I wanted to be a specialist. It took me a number of years to convince people that I was a trainer, not a handler."

At a water blind at the 1959 National in Reno, only two of the handlers could get their dogs to enter the water—not all that surprising, considering that the water was mostly ice. Rex thought to himself, "My dogs are going to go into the water."

Rex Carr's name rose to prominence in retriever circles in the 1960s after August Belmont shipped a Lab pup out to Escalon. Rex soon called Belmont to say, "Send more Super Chiefs. He makes the sun shine for me." Soupy did not stay in Rex's kennel. He slept in his bedroom. "Soupy was the most complete dog I've ever trained. It wouldn't have mattered if Scotland Yard used him or they had him run cattle or put him on the stage—that dog loved the world and everything in it. Dogs like that are few and far between."

"Rex was controversial," Belmont said, "because he refused to handle dogs in trials and only trained those who did. He was the first guy to use electronic collars—he experimented with the manufacturers. He was a maverick in the game but head and shoulders above all the others. Many people didn't hit it off with him, but it was a relief for me to get away from Wall Street and go out there every year and get ordered around for two weeks. He's not very tactful."

Rex used to bring his teams of clients to the Nationals and National Amateurs to train a full week ahead, exhausting bivouacs that continued right on through the trial. He rarely comes anymore—he made an exception for the 1991 National in Modesto, which was dedicated to him—but his influence hangs in the air like cordite.

"Carr is the most knowledgeable retriever man in the United States. He has no peer. He is short with his clients and better with his dogs."

"Rex is so hard to explain. At times he seems like he's on a different wave length. He tries to work through the dogs' heads, rather than beating them up."

"Timing of stimulation is what Rex teaches. He really reads dogs."

"Rex has the personality of a good Lab: he doesn't hold a grudge. He's an intuitive trainer. Someone will bring a dog out to him, and we'll guess what he's going to do with that dog, and he'll do something off the wall that we'd never have dreamed of. And it works."

"Rex is an egomaniac. He never makes a mistake— the handler or the dog makes a mistake. He felt he had to break down both dogs and handlers and rebuild them. I saw a man who won a National crying like a baby after Rex got through with him at Escalon. But he was a great, great teacher."

Out on the stubble field clients were arranged in chairs beside Rex, waiting their turn. His exclamatory voice was as loud as a claxon.

"No! David! No~! Why did you do that?"

Dave Schilling, in pale green Bermuda shorts, white polo shirt, and sneakers, stood before Rex at the center of a "wagon wheel" of retrieving bumpers. His back was in spasm, and he stood in a pelvic tuck. He was holding an electronic transmitter in both hands at chest height in what Sweezey would describe as "the manner of prayer." He had already warmed up his Lab Piper by throwing short marks to the wagon wheel. Now on blind retrieves he was forcing Piper to run past these attractions to hidden piles of bumpers scattered around a pond. Piper reached the wheel and turned toward temptation. Schilling blew his whistle, squeezed the button, and shouted, "No!" Piper sat and yelped.

"Damn!" roared Rex, "You blew the whistle too late! You have to hit him the *moment* he turns toward that pile!"

Rex shifted in his chair and said, "Write this down and underline it. *When dogs make mistakes, don't hold it against the dog! Point the finger at yourself.* If you can keep from ever blaming the dog, you will be in the best possible frame of mind to train him. How many can train with their tongue between their teeth? They'd chew it off! They blame the dog for faults that are of the trainer's own making and then make the dog pay for it. You have to walk in the dog's shoes. You have to focus so hard on training that you sense what's happening before it happens. You have to concentrate on the dog, not the blind, not the mark, but the *dog*, and make that correction *now!*"

Rex stood up slowly. He used to hunt quail on horseback, a pointer out there finding the covey. He would shoot from the saddle, lean down, and accept the bird from the dog. Orthoscopic knee surgery has since finished his hunting.

"Now, I'm the dog," he said. "They shoot a flier and you see this." Leaning to one side, he moved his left foot slightly forward. "That first little step is the source of all creeping. You take care of that first step and correct it and you don't have to deal with creeping and breaking later. These trainers let something get out of hand, and then they butcher the dog. Who wants that?" Slowly he sat back down.

Rex admits to having been "pet happy" since he was a kid in Streeter, North Dakota. He would spend hours encouraging rabbits to follow him. Pigeons would sit on his head. Knowing when his hen was about to lay an egg, he would address the citizens of Streeter: I can make this hen lay. They would smile. Rex would reach underneath her and produce an egg. When the farmers came into Streeter, their dogs following the wagons, Rex would follow the dogs. A dilatory dog would end up at Rex's home. He would begin training.

"Take the dog back, Rex," his parents would say. Another wagon, another dog would come to town. "Take it back, Rex."

After the war Rex made a trip to Montana and bought a Lab pup. The dog's name was Rip. "That was an incredible dog. I did everything with him, stage and screen." The manager of the San Francisco Giants farm club in Fresno asked if Rex would put on a show at the stadium. Rex called for a volunteer. A small boy came down from the stands. Rex introduced him to Rip, asked the boy for his address, then had him scribble a note on a slip of paper, which Rex put into a capsule and attached to a homing pigeon. (Rex raised and raced homers.) Rex placed the homer in Rip's soft mouth. "Back!" Rip drove into deep center. Whistle. Rip sat. "Drop!" The pigeon flew off. When Rex got home, the homer was there with the note. He mailed the note to the boy. "I could do anything with that dog."

Among visitors who would come to Rex's grounds to watch the dog work was a wary blue heron. Rex decided to "cultivate" the bird. He sent a dog down a channel, driving a school of minnows toward shore. The heron was there, its toes in the water. Three times the beak shot down into the water. Three times the heron swallowed. The heron stayed around, persuaded that working retrievers performed a useful function. Herbie the Heron. Herbie would stand on the piles of bumpers, honoring. Herbie was steady.

Rex once coaxed a colt into his bedroom. The colt picked up a bedspread in its teeth, looked into the mirror, dropped the spread, and walked into the living room. Rex then carressed it into a hypnotic state. The colt, all legs, lay down on the floor. Soupy saw his chance for abundant warmth and lay against the colt's belly. Rex stretched out beside its back. A cat curled up on the rib cage. Rex has a photograph of the scene. The colt was asleep.

"She was content," he said. "Some of us have a way with animals. The woods are not full of us."

In the early 1950s Rex began "experimenting with electricity." He hooked a six-volt battery and a door buzzer to his belt and ran a cord with two electrodes up to the dog's collar: force training. When Sputnik II went up, he climbed to the top of a water tower to watch it winking across the evening sky. Rex said to himself, there's a dog up there being manipulated electronically. It made him realize that something like an electronic collar might be just around the corner.

As it happened, a few small companies were already developing such collars. Rex tried them all. He played with them, experimented, held them in his hands and turned on the juice—Yow!—gradually evolving his program of complete collar control. The companies sought his advice. They made pilgrimages to Escalon. They dropped his name, much to his anger.

"Godalmighty!" he said, "it was risky using those early collars. They were so crude, always malfunctioning. A motorcycle going by or an airplane flying over would set them off. People ruined a lot of dogs. But of course it was necessary for someone to pioneer. You can go back in *Sports Illustrated* and read John Olin condemning the collar. He was pointing his finger at me. He didn't say anything about how he used a shotgun to get his dogs to stop. There are plenty of pitfalls to the collar. It can and will be misused, but people will get more expert with it over time."

Few of them measure up to Rex's standards. "Trainers today don't train their dogs enough," he said. "They take shortcuts and try to cure everything with that button. Too many people look at the collar as a panacea. It isn't. You can punch a dog out too much and ruin him. Some people think they can do anything with a dog. They can't. Unless that dog has the potential, you can't put it there.

"I start with a system of commands. Some form of force is used by everyone to teach. But you should reduce it to a minimum until the dog learns the commands. Then you start applying pressure.

"Show me temperament in a person and I'll show you a similar one in a dog. You have to treat dogs as individuals. I've got a dog named Scooter—magnificent animal, incredible desire. He has such a high threshold for pain and pressure. You take another dog and administer the least amount of shock possible and he will scream bloody murder. Any animal—you, me, a dog—has a certain limit to the amount of pressure it can take without things going awry. What happens if you use force improperly in training your dog and he doesn't understand? Instead of delivering the bird, he may go out in the tules and bury it, or eat it. I call that rebellion. If you exceed that pressure, what's next? Insanity of the dog.

"It's impossible to make things too simple for the dog. Teach them first before you test them. Teach them over and over and over. I feel that with a young dog you should have three successes for every two poor performances. He needs that to build his confidence.

"All these trial dogs sooner or later get flier happy. Once the dog gets out there ninety yards or so, he's thinking 'Flier, flier!' and he'll even pull away from that popper bird nearby just to go get the flier. These dogs will be consistent, but only as long as you are consistent. How does Larry Bird do what he does? It's practice, practice, repetition, repetition. While the other guys are back there loafing in the locker room, he's out there practicing his shots. You get a form and you stick with it.

"If you don't love dogs, forget it. You can't hide your emotions from them. It's important to start your dogs in a good frame of mind and put them away at the end of the day in a good frame of mind. But there's a fine line between that and what too many people do. They overdo praise and lose the dog's respect. The dog is always probing you, always measuring you. Some of these dogs are thinkers. They're trying to think beyond you. You have to train them not to think but to submit."

·3·

*T*HE SECOND day of the 1988
National Championship Stake began at six in the morning with the air warm, humid, and moving. It nearly blew the Porta-Potties out of their chains and off the flatbed hauling relief to the trial. The grounds were still dark. A voice over the loudspeakers made this inquiry:

"May we have the guns please?"

There was a period of silence.

"Will the dead bird guns please report?"

Another long silence. The voice acquired a tone of urgency.

"Clive, could we have the guns, please?"

"As soon as they're here."

Dottie Metcalf stepped out of her van. She was wearing gum shoes and bluejeans. Rick Roberts sat under the dome light reading a newspaper. On the drive out from

Maryland, he had finished *The Closing of the American Mind*, and after running Riggo he would start on *The Cardinal of the Kremlin*. Somewhere back there in the van among their hanging clothes, Rick's newspapers, the pheasant crates, dog kennels, dog food, bowls, water jugs, guns, and other gear was *The Roaring Eighties* by Adam Smith. Rick's books, his newspapers, the Creek bow and arrows he bought in Oklahoma City, his "damned stuff," as Dottie would say, were always reappearing in new places in her van. Dottie was meticulous about her van, as she is about her appearance, trying without much success to keep ahead of Rick's methods of clutter.

Dottie opened the side and rear doors to give Riggo and Megan some ventilation, then asked Bill Schrader, a vet from Houston, if he knew what the front was doing.

"It extends from California through Canada. It's into Arizona and New Mexico, coming this way."

Rick pressed a transistor radio to his ear and said, "El Paso is reporting forty-six-mile-an-hour winds. Oklahoma City has twenty-three."

"These winds here are every bit of twenty-three."

Schrader was supplying the National and the handlers with trial and training birds. He was built like a catcher. He once drove racing cars. He had driven up to Ardmore the previous week to train for the National with Rick, Dottie, and the Aycocks, towing behind his truck a small trailer holding a three-wheel off-road vehicle—it resembled a Big Wheel with knobby balloon tires. In training, they had moved bird crates by ORV and communicated from line to gun with radio headsets.

Schrader would be running Trumarc's Dizzy a few dogs ahead of Rick and Riggo. He was worried about the dogs being able to see the birds.

"I think we'll have better light when we run than if we had run last night," Rick said.

"We're in luck if we've got Max Phillipi on that popper, because he can throw that sucker a mile."

The three of them walked down to the line to watch the test dogs run. When the birds went up, all that was visible was the orange flash from the guns. When they returned to the van, Roberts said to Schrader, "They ought to wait about twenty minutes to start."

"Those hens are hard to see against that hill."

Rick slipped a white bib—number 85—over his head and walked down to the gallery. Clive Ostenberg, captain of the guns, told him that he had delivered up all his jokes on Sunday and had heard them ten times since. Rick attempted some small talk with Ostenberg, but his mind was on the light, the wind, on Riggo. Being the last dog, Riggo had spent the first day of the National in the crate, listening to the loudspeaker, whistles, and gunfire. Rick didn't want him too excited for this first series. He wanted him settled down, paying attention, ready to mark.

Hawkeye's Rocket was charging around in the brush on the hill trying to dig out the flier. Observing this, Rick swayed from side to side having sympathy pains.

"Oh, Rocket, oooh!"

Dottie Metcalf walked up. "Did he get it?"

"Yeah, but he had a big rangy hunt."

Schrader soon was up with Dizzy. As Dizzy came out of the gullies, Dottie said, "He's getting rangy."

Roberts was in labor. "Ah, God! *No!* Oh, Diz. He's way over."

On the memory bird, Dizzy ran far right of the fall, drove deep up the hill above the bird, and then swung left to the ponds and disappeared behind the willows.

"Oh God, Diz! Oh *no!*"

Rick turned in a little circle, his head down, his hands in his hip pockets. He looked back at Diz. "This is the time when you say to yourself, 'Why didn't I go out this morning and throw something to settle him down?'"

Trumarc's Dizzy finally turned and ran back to the fall. In the high grass he found the pheasant.

"Why do they do that?" Rick said. "They take this giant blow and then come back as if they knew it was there all along."

Schrader put Diz on the blind bird in two whistles and walked him back to the truck. "The flier didn't break the skyline," he said to Rick. "I knew Diz hadn't seen the bird. He didn't bring his ears up or anything. I thought of putting my hand down and giving him a line, but I was afraid he'd think it was a blind, and then I'd have to be handling him on a mark."

Rick opened Riggo's crate in the rear of the van, and the dog leaped out, tail wagging. Riggo shook himself. His ears flapped like a sheet on the line. He looked up at Rick, a "Yahoo!" expression on his face. He was panting, animated, all cranked up.

"Heel, Riggo, *heel!*" Rick was anxious, and there was an edge to his voice. He walked Riggo to the airing area behind the vehicles and let him romp around and relieve himself.

Rick slipped a chain collar over Riggo's thick neck. A short leather lead was permanently fastened to the chain so that he would not forget to remove it when they went to the line. Other than the whistles hanging from their necks, handlers are not allowed to "carry exposed any training equipment," including lead and collar, to the line. Dottie, who dislikes bulky coat pockets, goes to the line with the lead in one pocket, the chain in the other. At a trial once, she tucked the lead away and didn't realize the collar was still on the dog until she put her hand down to send him for the birds. The judges disqualified the dog.

Rick and Riggo headed for the holding blinds. The wind was picking up, driving the dogs left of the birds. Sweet Freezout Fancy blew clear over the dam. The radio was reporting winds in the mountains around El Paso of one hundred and one.

Riggo's flier went low and tumbled behind scrub trees. He raced out and nailed the bird.

Dottie sighed. "One down."

Rick lined up Riggo for the memory bird and said, "Riggo!" The dog flew out of the gullies considerably right of the fall. Dottie stiffened.

"Oooooh, he's going right!"

Riggo looked left and swung to the bird. Dottie relaxed, said he was a super dog, wondered if Rick had purposely pulled him right.

Riggo took three casts to the blind, was about to overrun the bird when Rick whistled him to a sit. The bird was just behind the dog, over his left shoulder. Riggo's spin would be enough to angle him there. At three hundred yards, Riggo looked like a small black stump. Rick's right arm went up.

"Back!" Riggo spun and jumped on the pheasant.

"It's a lot easier handling than watching," Dottie said.

Rick walked Riggo over to where a photographer for the *Retriever Field Trial News* was taking pictures of the handlers and dogs returning from the line. He knelt in the grass for the obligatory pose by the sitting retriever.

"Heel! *Heel!*"

Riggo was not heeling. He was not sitting. Riggo was deliriously deaf. He rolled on his back, kicking his legs in the air, rubbing against Oklahoma. Rick almost fell over laughing.

Rick put Riggo back into his crate and sat down in the van. "God, I hate these first series. You know all the things that can go wrong. That wind gets up your butt and you're gone."

Only nine dogs were dropped. Rick, Dottie, Schrader, the Aycocks (Judy's husband was also running a dog), and Sweezey were still in.

Rick and Dottie drove off to do their laundry. There were hen pheasants in a plastic crate in the van. The van smelled of coop. They would touch up Megan with some fliers.

The trial moved to another ranch for the more complicated third and fourth tests: a triple water mark with an honor and a water blind.

In the early days of field trials, the honor part of the test demanded exceptional steadiness. The honor dog, having retrieved, had to sit quietly by and watch three retrievers work consecutively on birds through completion. Non-slip retrievers.

Today the dog returns from his last retrieve, delivers the bird, and sits on the honor pad while the next dog comes up. As soon as that dog takes off for his first bird, the honor dog and handler walk off. Some honor.

The line was placed back from the shallow end of a large stock pond. The marks would be across the left bank of the pond. The shoreline was indented with points and inlets. The dogs would have to drive across numerous interdictions of land and water to get the birds. They would be running through shallows ("running water") into chest-high water ("lunge water"), then swimming the deeper water ("swimming water") to hold their lines to the birds. The flier, a tempting hen mallard, was the center bird, about one hundred and sixty yards deep up a hill, flanked lower down the incline by two shorter poppers. The shooting order was left, center, right. The flier would be tempting bait. Go for the deep flier first and you might have trouble checking down your dog for the short birds. Go for a popper first and the dog might get out there and opt for the flier. Bait and switch. You're out.

If Roberts had been concerned early that morning about the wind, here he would have to contend with air of considerably greater torque. The National Weather Service warned of tornados. Bricks anchored the line and honor mats, and the wind made those standing in the gallery take involuntary steps forward.

Just before noon the temperature suddenly dropped, and the sky turned green. The clouds swooping low overhead were bellied and ominous. Huge drops of rain began splattering the ground as the black front burst over the National with a cannonade of heavy millimeter hail. I jumped into the nearest truck with a Texan named Mac McGee. The judges dived under the upended canvas of a holding blind; under there with them were two handlers and their Labs.

Weather rarely delays a field trial and almost never cancels one. An arriving hurricane once disrupted a field trial near Boston, driving Rick and Patti Roberts all the way to Albany seeking safety for their dogs. They called Boston. The trial would resume. They drove back and ran their dogs.

When the storm passed, the guns were taking their positions in hail slush. The judges were in their chairs. Their scoring sheets were waterproof. A bolt of lightning lit the sky. The birds went up, and the dog went out.

Shifting from the south, the wind then blew out of the west, pushing some of surficial New Mexico and Texas before it. The dust storm soon drove us back to McGee's truck. Paper plates flew like sea gulls into the pond, which had taken on the appearance of chocolate.

"All we need now," said McGee, "is snow tonight and locusts tomorrow."

Diz had trouble finding the flier, and Schrader had to use his whistle. On the deeper popper, the memory bird nearest the shore, Diz swam past the guns the length of the lake and disappeared over the dam. Jay Sweezey, Dottie Metcalf, and the Aycocks stood together in empathy. After a successful test, handlers find a path back to their truck that intersects the gallery. A bad test and they detour. Schrader, shaking his head, did not stop to talk.

Riggo hit the water like a catapulted torpedo. He swam hard, his powerful shoulders lunging forward with each stroke. He picked up the left popper, but he hunted so long for the flier that Rick had to handle him to the bird.

The last popper was beyond coordinate memory. Riggo went into the water right of the course that would take him to the bird and began swimming down the middle of the lake. Rick stood with his legs apart, his hands cupped around the whistle, blowing in defeat. Rick's rule is that when you see a handler put his hands on his hips, you know he's had it. Rick had his hands on his hips.

They walked back from the lake, Riggo panting, dripping wet, tail wagging. Riggo appeared to be entirely delighted. Rick smiled in resignation. "God, what a way to make a living."

"The wind did you in, pardner," Sweezey said.

"He got so far out in the water on that third bird, he thought he was going for a blind."

"I saw that. This wind is so hard we've got whitecaps."

"Well, I'll cross another state off my list," Dottie said. "We did have a good fall, Rick."

"It was a good fall. You lose your sense of humor at the National and you might as well hang it up."

A brown curtain of dust rimmed the entire horizon. In nearby Comanche, the wind threw a roof into the street.

The National is a long play of successive little dramas, stretched out in repetitive acts as seventy or eighty dogs come to the line and do their solos. The next day maybe sixty do it. The next, maybe forty, as the field narrows and the tests toughen. Eight to ten hours of boredom and a few minutes of panic, handlers say. They all want badly to survive the cuts, to win against unbankable odds and the quirkiness of the elements.

"I don't know how many of these I've been to," Rick said, slumping in the seat of Dottie's van, "but I'll say this: the wind is your enemy. It just kills you. As badly as Riggo does in the wind, he really tried his best. Those dogs who ran before this front came in were having no trouble. Now look at them. Oh, Jesus! Look at Rocky!"

Rocky was Mioak's Main Event, a Golden Retriever who had by now forgotten his mark and was running down the dam and out of the National. His handler was Bill Eckett, who, with different dogs, had won the National in 1987 and the Canadian National just two months before this one. The wind was killing him. Rocky would be absent from the call backs.

Darkness arrived before all the dogs could be run on the marks. Megan would run this test in the morning. She would have to be perfect to stay in.

On Wednesday morning, day three, the first dogs ran before dawn. The gallery sat bundled up in their vehicles with the engines running, white exhaust rising in the air. It felt like winter.

Judy Aycock walked Cody to the line. Judy had an athlete's walk. She was trim and attractive, her short blond hair barely visible beneath a white cap. As a young girl growing up in Winnetka, Illinois, she had competed in AKC obedience trials with her poodle, then later with shelties when pursuing her degree at UCLA. Obedience trials, however, did not hold her competitive interest. ("You take a real clunk and you can be half-assed competitive in obedience trials, but not in this game.") She had read James Lamb Free's book and started attending retriever trials, where she learned that Super Chief was "the hottest thing going" and that a man by the name of Rex Carr had trained him. She began making weekend commutes from Los Angeles to Escalon. Eventually Judy moved there, rented a house, and for a number of years intermittently trained "sunup to sundown" with Carr.

"It didn't take her long to have a big influence on this sport," Rick said, watching Judy and Cody over the dashboard of Dottie's warm van. "Judy's record is hard to beat. The most successful dog in the history of this game was River Oaks Corky. In his career he had over five hundred points in stakes awarding championship points. Cody is second highest. There's a lot of jealousy in this business, particularly toward Judy. She is very reserved and shy, which some mistake for snobbery. But she isn't snobbish."

After picking up his first two birds, Cody was having difficulty remembering the fall of the third one. He went over the distant dam and out of sight. Judy stood still looking across the lake, hoping he would hunt his way back to the bird without a handle. After a long wait, her arms dropped to her sides. She blew her come-in call—beep, beep, beep, beep. Cody reappeared. He hunted to the bird, but he had been handled on a mark. The judges had their heads down making notes. Cody could have no more mistakes.

Sweezey followed with Smokey, and Smokey blew over the dam. He would survive the call-backs, but he too had no room for further error.

Dottie opened the rear doors. "Come on, Meggie, this is it."

She came to the line and called for the birds. As the guns fired, Roberts threw his head back in dispair.

"Aahhh, God! Megan's looking away! Come on, Megan. Oh, Meggie, *come on!*"

Megan came out of the water and hunted for the popper. She looped, she quartered, extending her range in widening transects that began carrying her in dangerous proximity to the flier. Once committed to the popper, she would be eliminated if she then switched birds.

"Oh, Christ! She's going to go for the flier!"

Dottie's whistle shrieked. She stepped sharply to the left, leaned, threw both her arms out at nine o'clock, and shouted, "*Over!*" Megan finally got the message, turned and bounded down the hill, picked up the popper pheasant, and returned with it in her mouth.

Dottie appeared to be about to send Megan when she turned and walked her over to the honor pad. Rick was perplexed. "*Now* what's happening?" The guns walked out to pick up the birds. Megan had been disqualified.

Rick walked out to meet Dottie as she returned with Megan to the van.

"Jesus Christ! What was *that* all about?"

Dottie's eyes widened. "Didn't you *see* it? I sent her for the flier and she didn't go. I put my hand down, and she went out a few feet and turned around. She didn't know where she was!"

Rick folded his arms, his voice low. "You've got to walk in the dog's shoes. That was what we talked about last night. When you handled her off that flier, you were telling her she didn't belong there. Then you sent her right back there. How do you explain that to the dog?"

The two of them stood side by side, discussing whether Dottie should have sent Megan for the bird to the right. Roberts suddenly pointed in the direction of a black Lab running up the hill. "Look at that dog! He's doing just what Megan did, switching to the flier and refusing handles. Piper's Pacer. He won the Canadian National. Explain *that!* How could two dogs in a row do what seventy dogs have not? And then to have two dogs in a row—Cody and Smokey—go over the hill? You tell me. We need a dog psychologist here to explain why these dogs do what they do. At the end of this trial a very good dog will win it, but a number of very good dogs will be made to look awful."

Ten dogs were not called back, including Dizzy, Megan, and Riggo. For the rest of this National, Rick, Dottie, and Schrader would be in the gallery. Cody would run the water blind. So would Smokey and B. B.

For the blind, the fourth test, the line was pulled even farther away from the water's edge. The dogs would have what the handlers called a "long land entry" to the pond—a significant obstacle in itself—and then, hugging the right shore but not landing on it, they would have to charge through shallow water, go over a point, swim a bay and past another inviting point to a dead duck planted two hundred and twenty-five yards from the line. Running water, lunge water, and swimming water. The wind, having picked up and now quartering from the right, could push dogs into open water and make it difficult for the handlers to keep them close to the shore. The nearness of the shore would invite the dogs to dock, and once on land they would resist being recast into the water. Obstacles.

Tommy Sorenson, a seasoned pro from Missouri who trains and handles dogs for Audrey Wallace, a St. Louis Busch, was in the holding blind, and he knew he was in trouble. FC Watermelon Man—nicknamed Amos—was clacking his teeth, "just chomping up a storm," and foaming at the mouth. Sorenson was not concerned about epilepsy. He suspected that a bitch ahead of Amos was in season. In the early years of Nationals, the female dogs were examined for estrus every day of the trial. Now checks are made the day before the National opens and only later if the handler requests it or someone complains. This was an awkward time to complain if one were not sure.

When Sorenson put his hand down and said "Back!" Amos was not thinking bird. He trailed to the water with his nose down and fooled around. Amos was aroused. He was making a bird's nest of a straight line. Sorenson blew his whistle. Amos wasn't listening. He blew again, gave Amos an over. Amos wasn't going over. On the third whistle, Sorenson got him on land and recast him. Amos went back into the water, took three more whistles, and reached the duck.

The dog that had run before Amos was Risky Business Jem. The following day, the handler in Amos's absent slot could not get his dog's nose off the ground in the holding blind. He went to the trial committee. Jem was found to be in heat. Jem was scratched. Obstacles.

Judy Aycock sat in the last holding blind with Cody's head in her lap. She bent over and examined his eyes. She blew into them softly, wiping carefully with her thumbs, and patted him on the head. She walked Cody to the line, put her hand down, and said, "Back!" Judy was determined to keep Cody in the water and past the inviting point. Other dogs had docked and refused to reenter.

Cody picked up speed through the grass, went straight into the shallows, and slowed. Judy recast him, and he set off swimming. He passed the point and did not disembark. Probably scenting the bird, he began pulling toward shore. Judy's depth perception was off. Thinking he was docking early, she blew her whistle. Cody spun and faced her, treading water. "Back!" He went back, past the bird. Judy realized her error and began blowing her whistle, but Cody was in lunge water, lunging, unable to hear her for all the sucking and splashing of water. He lunged on as he had been cast, beyond the bird. In swimming water he finally heard her whistle, handled to the shore, and came back to the bird.

The water blind would scuttle eighteen retrievers, Cody and Amos among them. Some dogs had refused to go into the lake at all. They had to be picked up by their handlers—disqualified.

Smokey and B. B. stayed in. Sweezey pulled on a bright green windbreaker and drove off to air and feed his dogs.

On Thursday the Doobissary was parked in a grove of oaks on the edge of a big open meadow, site of tests five and six. The guns lunched on grilled pheasant salad and Zapp's potato chips. The gallery bent toward the aroma in the trees, and handlers with time to spare and jerky between their teeth drifted toward the Doobissary.

The fifth series—triple land marks—included an honor and a retired gun on a weedy dike at the left. Tommy Sorenson, his silver pompadour making a standing wave over his wide, cheerful face, watched Sweezey send Smokey.

"I'd like us to get back to more natural ability," Sorenson said, "so you see marks without needing binoculars. At the National, the judges should be lenient. You train all year and spend thousands of dollars. They usually give you two mistakes, but I would go for four. What the hell, the judges have got their notes on every dog. Let the dogs play."

Smokey made it through his marks, and a few hours later Sweezey sent B. B. Powder. As B. B. returned to Sweezey's trailer, the judges wrote "excellent" on their sheets.

Bob Sibley was on break. He stepped from the Doobissary as a handler at the line called for the birds. The flier appeared to be getting away. Sibley, who admits to finding "these tests of black dogs rather boring," is nevertheless serious about his shooting. As the pheasant approached the limits of twelve-gauge range, Sibley was professionally alarmed.

"Jesus! Shoot that sonofabitch!"

The pheasant fell well beyond the circle.

"That's what we call an LFF. A long fucking fall."

Big River Bonne Amie, former Canadian National Field Champion, was hopping around at the line. She seemed about to slip. Another gun on break said, "In the old days, that dog would be out for doing that. But to get a dog to 'sit quietly' as the rules require takes a lot of control and can take a lot out of a dog like this."

Handlers have employed all sorts of subterfuge to steady their dogs at the line. Jay Sweezey used to put his hand in his pocket and draw his thumb over the teeth of a comb. "It was a warning," he said. "Chuck Morgan used to sneeze. When Cliff Wallace was honoring with a hyper dog, he would snap his Zippo lighter. I talk to my dogs all the time. I'll say 'easy' to get them to settle down. You're downwind of the judges, it's raining, they have their hoods up. They can't hear it."

For the sixth test, the dogs would have to hold a tight line across broken meadow past a distracting gun sitting in a chair (he would not shoot) to a deep blind two hundred eighty yards away. The bird was placed near where the flier gun team had recently stood, the residual scent from crates of live pheasants remaining to draw dogs into error. Well up the hill from the blind bird sat the bird planters behind a canvas blind of their own.

Little Duke of Fargo barreled past the blind bird, finally heard the whistle, and sat. Dean Troyer blew the come-in call as he pointed down. Duke was so far away that he saw Troyer's movement and was up to the bird planters before the sound of the whistle reached him.

"With so much momentum," Rick Roberts said, "he was going to go farther back if he saw *any* movement. Dean will never dig him out of those bird boys now." Little Duke of Fargo was dropped. The following summer he would win the National Amateur.

Jay Sweezey came up with Smokey. Smokey nailed the blind.

B. B. ran with such momentum that Roberts feared she would carry up to the bird planters.

"Come on, Sweez, hit her with the whistle." Rick moved his hips as though he was trying to drop a long putt. "Ooooo.......that's *it*."

Sweezey didn't move. He blew the come-in, and B. B. ran back down to the bird.

Thirty-one dogs, including Smokey and B. B., were in the call-backs for the next day.

Friday. Another front had arrived overnight, and it was cold and drizzling.

B. B. was in deep kimchi. The seventh test—triple water marks—was in rough cover, a hillside of burned-over timber and high brush and grass. A pond lay between the dogs and the birds. The dogs would swim ninety yards across the pond to a mallard duck shot close to the far shore. They then would splash through shallows to go for a pheasant flier on the left shot over brush and dead timber. The last bird was a deep popper far up the hill, the guns there retiring after the throw.

After getting the duck, B. B. had a long and exasperating hunt for the flier pheasant. When she finally returned with it, Sweezey expected her to be down and discouraged, but she went right back out and nailed the deep popper. The gallery applauded, their insulated gloves making a sound like fluttering wings. But the long hunt had hurt B. B. On that series, the judges marked her "weak."

"She had a really bad hunt on that pheasant," Tony Snow said later, "as a lot of dogs did. We call that a mixed-bag test, having them go for a nice warm duck and then go over for a pheasant. Because of its scent, a duck is a powerful influence on those dogs, particularly a freshly shot one. They go over for that other flier, maybe they smell pheasant, but they're looking for a duck. They have their duck nose on, not their pheasant nose. They're convinced that there is a warm duck in there. It's just like cocaine to them. They really like that hot duck."

B. B. improved somewhat on the eighth test, a water blind across the same pond. The line of departure was swung to the left and far back from the water, so that the course to the blind intersected the retrieves on the previous marks. A gun sat in a chair at the shore where the dogs would enter the water. He fired a "dry pop" (no bird thrown) just before each dog was released. The dogs had to run past the dry pop and into the water, then swim through a profusion of dead tree limbs while hugging the left shoreline, ignoring the attractions of land, their previous marks, their memory of hot mallard. Two hundred and twenty-five yards to a cold duck.

The water blind took Smokey out of the competition. B. B. received a "fair" in the judges' notes. Fifteen dogs were called back. B. B. was still in.

On Saturday, the last day of the National, there were handlers (and a writer) who would have preferred to stay in bed. A winter storm was coming in from the west, and its leading edge was cold rain driven by an insistent wind and illustrated by lightning. Snow was approaching the Oklahoma Panhandle. Duck weather.

The ninth test was a quad—four water marks—across a narrow lake full of dead trees and surrounded by an oak forest that dropped over steep banks into the water. The clay road into the ranch was red gumbo. My car slid down the hill, and I parked beside a solitary pump jack. Texaco Well No. 1, Sec. 36 IS 73. Pup-pup-pup-pup-pup-pup-pup. It was pumping in the rain, incongruous for this engagement of dogs but not for this state.

Clive Ostenberg had sought comfort in the hostess committee's RV, and I followed him in. There was coffee there, and Clive topped his up with a touch of whiskey. If I thought this weather was bad (and I did), he wanted me to know that the first National was held in late December on Long Island, that after casing his gun at the conclusion of the 1980 National in Roswell, New Mexico, he drove out through a foot of snow; and that six years later in St. Louis, with the temperature around seven degrees, they had to break ice so that the dogs could swim blinds. Each year as it switches time zones, the National migrates farther south and a bit earlier in November. The next year it would return to Georgia.

Barbour rain gear, dressed with waterproofing gook, was in evidence in the gallery, such as it was, a diminished squad of standing masochists, among them Rick Roberts. Rick didn't like grease on his clothes. He was in electric blue Gortex, crinkling audibly with every move in the cold. He would undoubtedly go to the next National, but it was not to his liking to see the National Champion Retriever coming out of a milieu of swamp gas and fog.

"If the purpose of field trials is to test retrievers to do what they're bred to do," he said, "they should be tested in ducking weather, and that's cold weather and cold water. It's not telling you much about the quality of a retriever if he's running south Georgia. One year a dog who won the National Amateur in June would not get into the water on a mark at the National in St. Louis. He had to be handled into the water. It took multiple handles, and I'm not sure if he ever did go in. The National should weed those dogs out. If run on a blind from the edge of the water, most dogs will go in. But the real test is to back them up a long way from the water and then send them. It's a hell of a thing to ask of a dog, and a lot of dogs won't do it. A really cold water blind is the ultimate test. I don't like cold weather, but a National Champion ought to get his bird out of cold water."

The wind had shifted one hundred eighty degrees from the test setup a week earlier. The judges flipped the test to run with the wind, switching the line and guns to opposite banks of the gloomiest looking setting one could imagine for a trial. It was cold weather. It was cold water.

The line was on a steep bank, the birds thrown into aggravations of swamp and brush. Three poppers (one retired) and a flier. The thrower for one of the marks had to toss from a pitching boat to the shore, but he was off balance, missed the shore, and splashed some ducks into the shallows. A splashed bird would be easier to mark.

"No bird," said the judges, and the dogs on the line had to be taken back to their trucks and rerun later.

Field trialers fear "no bird," especially a poorly hit flier near the end of the National when the dogs are cranked up by a week of shooting, fliers, retrieving, and the absence of correction. The dog sees the bird go up—his adrenalin about to vaporize—and is then put away. Retrievus interruptus. He remembers. On the rerun, he often ignores the new bird and goes out and hunts for "no bird." It had happened to Jay Sweezey in the finals of the 1966 National. His dog got a no-bird flier and had to wait for five dogs before rerunning. When he sent the dog again, she ignored the flier before her eyes and ran to where she had seen the original one go down. No bird.

Some dogs quit. Tommy Sorenson and FC Travelin Light had a no-bird and were dropped on the rerun. "It was too bad," Sorenson said, as he stood in the rain watching Sweezey. "He's a real sensitive dog. The judge said, 'No!' and his ears went down. I couldn't get him up again."

The other handlers just worried about their retrievers being higher than kites and the string snapping. At the conclusion of the 1976 National, Rex Carr had some intelligence that Judy Aycock's San Joaquin Honcho might have clinched it. Suggesting to Judy that she might want to spruce up some before the award ceremonies, Rex sent another handler, Don Weiss, down to her truck to get Honcho. Weiss did not return. Rex found him engaged with the dog. The National Champion Retriever was so excited he had leaped up on Weiss, a big Shreveport lawyer, and pinned him in a bear hug. Weiss couldn't move.

B. B. was wired. She practically bolted from the holding blind, her head snapping from gun to gun in the watery gloom.

"*Heel!*"

B. B. sat on the line in metaphor only. Her tail swept the pad as the first bird went up. The second bird brought her butt off the ground. By bird four, she was nearly in front of Sweezey, crouching low to the ground. Sweezey stood hunched over, his legs slightly apart, his hands at his sides. Rick said of B. B., "She would break down a door to retrieve."

B. B. hit the water in a racer's leap, flat out, head forward, the spray flying. Swimming strongly, she collected the first three birds in successive retrieves and went for the flier, across the lake and up the hill, got it and swam back. As Sweezey and B. B. came off the line, the demi-gallery, huddled in the driving rain, gave insulated applause. Plup, plup, plup, plup. Sweezey smiled broadly. He was wearing the tan cap with the green bow.

The judges rated B. B. "good." Three dogs were dropped. B. B. had been a finalist in the 1986 National, and she would be one of the dozen finalists in this one.

The tenth and final test of the National Championship Stake finished at midafternoon in the rain. The gun teams were soaked, and so were the throwers, the handlers, the dogs, and the birds.

Sweezey and B. B. came to the line at the crest of a sweeping pasture that fell away into lateral drainage and rose up a long hill. He was wearing a blue cap with a white bow. The test: a hen pheasant flier two hundred yards to the left. A popper bird nearly three hundred and fifty yards straight away, up the facing hill, and across a mud road. A cock pheasant flier to the right at the base of the hill, one hundred fifty yards out. Wet pheasants have difficulty flying fast. The right flier fell short, near the guns. No bird. B. B. and Sweezey walked back to the trailer to think about it.

On B. B.'s rerun, the flier on the right fell long to the left. B. B. raced down the hill, put a little hunt on between the bird and the old fall, and came up with the pheasant. Sweezey put her away in the trailer, switched to his tan cap with the green bow, and drove down to the ranch house where the winner would be announced.

The chili and sandwiches were gone before the judges arrived to present the winner: PP's Lucky's Super Toby, a black male Lab, handled by one of his owners, Charley Hays, an amateur. Hays put Toby on the table beside the winner's trophy and kissed him on the snout. Toby didn't mind the kiss, but he did not look all that comfortable on the table.

Sweezey congratulated Hays and shook his hand. Snow and hail were reported nearing Oklahoma City, and the reception soon broke up.

Sweezey got into his truck and drove south toward his son's kennel in Texas. There were big plugs of red Oklahoma mud on his trailer hitch. He had to take care of his dogs.